CULTURE OF CUISINE

A THESIS ON
CULINARY IDEALS

BY
MICHAEL BENNETT

THE AUTHOR OF:
IN THE LAND OF MISFITS, PIRATES AND COOKS
AND
UNDERNEATH A CLOUDLESS SKY

PUBLISHED BY:
THE PROFESSIONAL IMAGE, INC.
　　　IN THE U.S: SOUTH BEACH AND SOUTH FLORIDA
　　　INTERNATIONAL: ST. CROIX, ST. THOMAS, TORTOLA, ST. MAARTEN, ARUBA

CONTACT US AT: THE_PROFESSIONAL_IMAGE@YAHOO.COM

"CULTURE OF CUISINE"
VOLUME ONE - "IDEALS"
FIRST OF THREE VOLUMES

ISBN: 978-1--450-78300-2

THANKS TO OUR STAFF:
SENIOR EDITOR: EILEEN CLARK
ASSISTANT EDITOR: JESS "E"
PHOTOGRAPHS: THE PROFESSIONAL IMAGE, INC.

WEBLINK TO OUR EMAIL.

COPYRIGHT © 2011 BY MICHAEL BENNETT~THE TROPICAL CUISINIER! ALL RIGHTS RESERVED. NO PART OF THIS PUBLICATION MAY BE REPRODUCED, DISTRIBUTED, OR TRANSMITTED IN ANY FORM OR BY ANY MEANS, INCLUDING PHOTOCOPYING, RECORDING, OR OTHER ELECTRONIC OR MECHANICAL METHODS, WITHOUT THE PRIOR WRITTEN PERMISSION OF THE PUBLISHER, EXCEPT IN THE CASE OF BRIEF QUOTATIONS EMBODIED IN CRITICAL REVIEWS AND CERTAIN OTHER NON-COMMERCIAL USES PERMITTED BY COPYRIGHT LAW. FOR PERMISSION REQUESTS, WRITE TO THE PUBLISHER, ADDRESSED "ATTENTION: PERMISSIONS COORDINATOR," AT THE ADDRESS BELOW.

THE PROFESSIONAL IMAGE, INC.
~SOUTH FLORIDA~
1720 HARRISON ST.
SUITE 11-E
HOLLYWOOD, FL. 33020

ORDERING INFORMATION:
QUANTITY SALES: SPECIAL DISCOUNTS ARE AVAILABLE ON QUANTITY PURCHASES BY CORPORATIONS, ASSOCIATIONS, AND OTHERS. FOR DETAILS, CONTACT THE PUBLISHER AT THE ADDRESS ABOVE. ORDERS BY U.S. TRADE BOOKSTORES AND WHOLESALERS. PLEASE CONTACT TPI DISTRIBUTION: TEL: 305-851-3441 OR, FOODBRAT@GMAIL.COM

QR CODE ENABLED BOOK

PRINTED IN THE UNITED STATES OF AMERICA

DEDICATION PAGE:

I'D LIKE TO TAKE YOU THROUGH A JOURNEY OF DAILY COMPETITION, STRIFE AND GRANDEUR.

As any chef will tell you, "This is the hardest job that I ever loved." For most chefs, this is true. Culinarians are a special breed of people. They take a raw food and transform it into art under spartan circumstances.

Being a chef is at times unsettling, and some people will never know that as chefs....

- It is the turmoil - that drives us.
- It is the heat and the frustration - that recharges us.
- It is the never-ending and daunting expectations - that drive us to perfection.
- It is the lack of surrounding culture - that makes us want to slice, weave and tie *edible works of art* into a Mozart-*like* concert.
- It is the lack of understanding - that makes us want to educate further.
- It is the infinite - that drives us to calculated singularism.

Innovation arises with the passage of time and countless hours of experimentation.

.....TO ALL THAT *I* HAVE WORKED WITH IN THE PAST AND TO EVERYONE THAT HAS SHAPED MY CULINARY VOICE - **THANKS.**

TRIBUTE TO SOUTH FLORIDA CHEFS

A TRIBUTE AND TIME LINE TO THOSE THAT MADE MIAMI AND SOUTH FLORIDA COOKERY A HOUSEHOLD WORD....

THIS TIME LINE SHOULD GIVE AN IDEA OF WHEN SOME OF OUR FAMILIAR VETERAN CHEFS FIRST CAME UPON THE STAGE -- AND IF/WHEN THEY OPENED A PLACE OF THEIR OWN.

TAKEN FROM THE LOCAL MIAMI RESTAURANT NEWSPAPER, NEW TIMES...

1986: ALLEN SUSSER OPENS CHEF ALLEN'S IN AVENTURA.
1986: DEWEY LOSASSO GAINS NOTICE AS CHEF OF THE FOUNDLINGS CLUB IN MIAMI BEACH.
1988: MARK MILITELLO OPENS MARK'S PLACE IN NORTH MIAMI BEACH.
1989: DOUG RODRIGUEZ SPARKS NUEVO LATINO CUISINE AT YUCA IN CORAL GABLES.
1989: PASCAL OUDIN TURNS HEADS AS CHEF OF THE COLONNADE IN CORAL GABLES.
1991: NORMAN VAN AKEN COMES TO MIAMI AT A MANO IN THE BETSY ROSS HOTEL ON OCEAN DRIVE.
1993: JONATHAN EISMANN BRINGS PACIFIC TIME TO A STILL-UNDEVELOPED LINCOLN ROAD.
1994: ROBBIN HAAS MAKES THE NEW COLONY BISTRO ON OCEAN DRIVE THE HOTTEST SPOT IN TOWN.
1994: JAN JORGENSEN'S TWO CHEFS DEBUTS IN SOUTH MIAMI. IT IS STILL THERE.
1994: CINDY HUTSON AND DELIUS SHIRLEY OPEN NORMAN'S ON THE BEACH ON LINCOLN ROAD, THE PRECURSOR TO ORTANIQUE ON THE MILE.
1994: MICHAEL SCHWARTZ CO-LAUNCHES NEMO IN SOUTH BEACH.
1995: NORMAN VAN AKEN OPENS HIS FIRST ESTABLISHMENT, NORMAN'S RESTAURANT, IN CORAL GABLES.
1998: ROBBIN HAAS COMMANDS RED SQUARE IN SOUTH BEACH.
1999: PHILIPPE RUIZ BECOMES CHEF DE CUISINE AT PALME D'OR IN THE BILTMORE HOTEL. HE IS STILL THERE.
1999: KRIS WESSEL OPENS LIAISON ON ESPAÑOLA WAY IN SOUTH BEACH.
1999: CINDY HUTSON OPENS ORTANIQUE ON THE MILE IN CORAL GABLES.
2000: PASCAL OUDIN OPENS HIS OWN PASCAL'S ON PONCE IN CORAL GABLES.
2000: MICHELLE BERNSTEIN GETS LOTS MORE ATTENTION AT AZUL IN THE MANDARIN ORIENTAL.
2003: TIM ANDRIOLA DEBUTS TIMO IN SUNNY ISLES BEACH.
2003: ANDREA CURTO-RANDAZZO AND FRANK RANDAZZO DAZZLE WITH TALULA ON SOUTH BEACH.
2004: DEWEY LOSASSO OPENS NORTH ONE 10 AS A PIONEER IN MIAMI'S BISCAYNE CORRIDOR.
2005: MICHELLE BERNSTEIN OPENS MICHY'S AS A PIONEER OF THE MIAMI'S MIMO NEIGHBOURHOOD.
2007: MICHAEL SCHWARTZ OPENS MICHAEL'S GENUINE FOOD & DRINK.
2008: KRIS WESSEL OPENS RED LIGHT ON THE LITTLE RIVER IN MIMO.
2010: DEWEY LOSASSO RE-CHEFS THE FORGE, A FLAMBOYANT PIONEERING RESTAURANT ON MIAMI'S SOUTH BEACH.
2011: CHEF ALLEN'S CLOSES AND BRINGS TO AN END TO NEW WORLD CUISINE AND EVERYONE INVOLVED WITH MIAMI'S CULINARY WORLD IS SADDENED.

INTRODUCTION

IN AMERICA, MODERN CUISINE IS CONSTANTLY CHANGING.

INNOVATION IS THE LIFE BLOOD OF ANY SUCCESSFUL RESTAURANT CHEF. AS YOU INITIATE INNOVATION, YOU ARE CRAFTING AN IDEAL. THIS CONSTRUCTION OF IDEALS IS A TENACIOUS THOUGHT PROCESS. WHEN YOU *CRAFT A CUISINE* IT IS FIRST THOUGHT, FOLLOWED BY FINESSE, THEN PRODUCTION AND FINALLY REFINEMENT. CUISINE HAS ETERNALLY BEEN THOUGHT OF AS A TEMPORARY AND A CONTEMPORARY ART FORM. SO A CHEF HAS TO BE CONSTANTLY GROWING TOWARDS AUGMENTED CREATIVITY.

WITH IMPUT FROM GENERATIONS OF CREATIVE SOUTH FLORIDA CHEFS, THIS BOOK IS FOR ALL NEW AND EXPERIENCED CHEFS.

MODERN CUISINE IS A COEXISTENT THOUGHT PROCESS. THE **CULTURE OF A CUISINE** IS THE DETERMINATION OF BOUNDARIES TO WHAT WERE YOUR CULINARY LIMITS, THEN EXCEEDING THEM. ON THE NEW AMERICAN RIVIERA, THERE ARE NO TRANSVERSAL CULINARY BOUNDARIES. THIS IS A LAND OF EXPERIMENTATION, WHERE ANYTHING GOES AND USUALLY DOES. IT HAS NO START OR END. IT IS A CONTINUOUS FLOW OF CORPOREAL TOIL.

THIS ART FORM IS ONE OF ORAL AND VISUAL TRAINING. OUR TRAINING CANNOT BE ACCOMPLISHED JUST BY READING RECIPE INSTRUCTIONS. READING ALONE IT IS NOT POWERFUL ENOUGH FOR A CONSUMMATE DISCIPLINE. *REPETITION, REPETITION, REPETITION* IS THE ONLY WAY TO TEACH COOKERY TO OTHERS.

On the New American Riviera, daydreaming is a popular way to create. While shopping at the morning marketplace, looking over a multitude of tropical food choices, your mind wanders as the combinations of these exotic tastes whirl around on your internal taste canvas. While dreaming about the combinations, you need to organize cookery sequences that respect the vibe of the past, while blasting through stale and misused non-pivotal cookery alliances. Recipe development should tell a story of where we cook on this earth. Our recipes should establish and set an imagery of the place in which we create, live and work. For me it has always been locally harvested tropical foods that represent the cookery preferences of South Floridian chefs.

This is the hallmark of the cuisine that was created on the New American Riviera.

Like a musician, we use the major chords of centuries-old French Classical cuisine to base culinary techniques while formulating a new cookery standard into a *techno-house* (music) vogue. You should taste a dish in your mind before writing a road map (recipe) to the dish. This is where the understanding of taste-relationships can't just be handed down from Mom. It is from personal experiences and repetition that stimulates this to an unconscious, but naturally sanctioned process. Working with recipes over and over again while you are day dreaming about the physical process, the mind forms an opinion based upon previously utilized taste inter-relationships. Trial and error help structure the totality of a new taste concept. The conception must be harmonious - just like a symphony of musical notes. Evolving your personalized taste-balance, comparable to the term of "taste-variance", is the direction that Culinarians go for when developing new menu items. A taste-variance is that special combination of ingredients that make the unexperienced go: "Ah-Ha" and, "that is the missing ingredient that the sauce needed."

It is the notion of a new taste-variance that brings like-minded ingredients into a realm that might have seemed implausible just a week earlier. This modernistic taste-variance is why you have become known as a food artist.

Your Recipes

Artists must heal as well as produce every day. Healing is a duty akin to raising your children. You should guide recipe creation to meticulous correctness. Repetition brings with it a sense of creating a process of exactitude and velocity. As one replicates a recipe over and over again, preparation time is noticeably shortened. Steps are streamlined and a deft hand at acute seasoning is achieved. A chef has to shepherd the language of the recipe and ceaselessly refine them like children. Writing a recipe that can be duplicated precisely the way you composed it is an outgrowth of exactness. A chef has to be able to describe his cookery adaptations, boundless creativity and dynamic culinary practices onto paper. Healing a recipe, is a chef's perpetual artistic demeanour.

A SOUTH FLORIDA TWIST...

A DAILY PARADOX FOR CHEFS IS TO BALANCE EXOTIC TROPICAL FLAVORS, TEXTURES AND COMPREHENSION ON EACH NEW PLATE PRESENTATION.

THE SIMPLEST WAY TO ILLUSTRATE THIS IS WHEN AN ACIDIC SAUCE (ONE THAT CONSISTS OF...CITRUSY VINEGAR, KEY LIME FRUIT JUICE, CALAMODINE, ETC....) IS APPLIED TO BALANCE THE FATTINESS (FATS BEING A VERY GOOD CARRIER OF TASTE) ON A FILLET OF SEABASS. FATS NOT ONLY TRANSPORT TASTE TO THE PALATE, BUT THE SENSORY CELLS ON YOUR PALATE TELL YOUR BRAIN THAT THE FOOD YOU ARE EATING IS RICH. RICH FOODS ALSO AFFECT THE STOMACH AND HOW IT COMMUNICATES FULLNESS. FATS WILL DISSOLVE IN THE STOMACH AND COAT THE SENSORY RECEPTORS ON THE STOMACH LINING; THIS TRANSLATES TO THE BRAIN THAT YOUR STOMACH IS FULL. IT IS NOT FULL; THE COATED SENSORY RECEPTORS HAVE A LAYER OF OIL OVER THEM.

ANOTHER YIN AND YANG EXAMPLE OF CREATIVENESS IN THE KITCHEN WOULD BE WHEN A CHEF USES A CRISP TEXTURED ORANGE (CITRUS-SHARPNESS IN TASTE) FLAVORED COOKIE TO CRADLE A CUSTARDY AND SOFT ATEMOYA DESSERT. CHEFS BLEND COOKING APPLICATIONS TO EFFECT TEXTURES AND FLAVORINGS IN MANY WAYS. USING THE SWEET CAMBODIAN MANGO AND THE INTENSE HEAT OF A SCOTCH BONNET PEPPER IN OUR SALSAS AND CHUTNEYS IS ANOTHER EXAMPLE OF OUR BALANCING AND MIXING OF THE TRIGIDIMAL COOKERY EFFECTS.

ONCE YOU UNDERSTAND HOW AND THEN WHY COMMONPLACE FOODS INTERACT WITH EACH OTHER, YOU CAN THEN ADD A RELATIVELY UNKNOWN FOOD WITH SIMILAR CHARACTERISTICS TO SUBSTITUTE FOR ANY SIMILAR ITEM IN A RECIPE.

THINGS THAT ARE *NEW* TO US ARE MEASURED BY WHAT WE ALREADY KNOW. NOT BEING AFRAID TO EXPERIMENT AND USE UNKNOWN FOODS LETS YOU DISCOVER THE UNDERLYING CULINARY WONDERLAND THAT IS SOUTH FLORIDA.

WHAT IS IT THAT MAKES THE TEFLON-CITY WHAT IT IS TODAY?

BEING FASHIONABLY DIFFERENT!

THIS IS EASILY SEEN JUST IN THE INFLUX OF DIFFERING NEW RESTAURANT CONCEPTS. THE CONCEPT THAT IS MOST EASILY RECOGNIZED BY THEIR MENU OF INGREDIENTS IS THE SEAFOOD AND PAN-ASIAN INFLUENCED EATERIES.

ONE INGREDIENT ON THESE MENUS THAT IS FAST BECOMING MORE RECOGNIZABLE IS THE MANGO.

THE MANGO IS FAST BECOMING AS COMMON AS THE APPLE IN THE DAILY PANTRY OF *"CLEAVER-ESQUE"* SOUTH FLORIDIAN. WITH THE SAME EXCITEMENT THAT A MANGO IMPARTS ONTO THESE NEW MENUS, A FESTIVAL TO CELEBRATE THIS UNIQUE FOOD ITEM HAPPENS ANNUALLY IN SOUTH FLORIDA.

FAIRCHILD GARDENS HOSTS AN INTERNATIONAL MANGO FESTIVAL THAT IS AN ANNUALLY CORAL GABLES (A MIAMI SUBURB) EVENT. IT IS THE LARGEST EVENT OF ITS KIND IN THIS HEMISPHERE OF THE WORLD. THIS INTERNATIONAL EVENT HAPPENS ON THE SECOND WEEKEND IN JULY. THIS UNREPLICABLE EVENT IS PECULIAR UNTO SOUTH FLORIDA BECAUSE THEIR GARDEN IS RIPE WITH 130 DIFFERENT VARIETIES OF MANGO. DR. CAMPBELL, THE CURATOR OF THE GARDEN TRAVELS AROUND THE WORLD TO COLLECT THESE SPECIES AND RE-DEPOSIT THEM HERE IN SOUTH FLORIDA.

Dr. Campbell heads up a contingent of celebrity chefs that help bring in local Foodies for a *Horizontal Mango Tasting*, which is just like a horizontal wine tasting. The panel of four celebrity chefs and Dr. Campbell discuss the differing taste attributes of five varieties of mango. There was also a vertical tasting. The vertical tasting outlines the different taste and uses throughout its phases of ripeness, in one variety of mango.

Mangos and South Florida Chefs

"I have been doing this event for five years now with Dr. Campbell. Our audience really loves it", states one chef. In previous years Robbin Haas stole the show with his interpretations of how to eat a mango... "naked in the bathtub". 'Robbin always has something amusing to add to the panel's evaluations', says the Chef.

The audience loves the commentary provided about each mango variety. The audience even intensely take notes as the chefs describe the mango's taste, textures, and sexy attributes. A chef related, "One year my wife was looking over onto her neighbors' wristwatch to see what time it was, and she suddenly covered her notes protectively. She thought my wife was trying to steal those scribbled secrets." They are real mango-a-holics at these events. The King of Fruit deserves loyalty but these people are about to give up a virginal sacrifice for our cooking tips.

THIS BOOK

IS FOR ALL OF US IN THE

CULINARY PROFESSION.

Table of Contents:

INTRODUCTION..PAGE 7
    INTRO INTO THE WORLD OF A SOUTH FLORIDA CHEF..........PAGE 10

Chapter One:
    CULTURE OF A CUISINE...PAGE 17
    HOW OUR CUISINE WAS CRAFTED..................................PAGE 18
    ODE TO FLORIDA, *CULINARY WASTELAND OR DREAMLAND*.....PAGE 20

Chapter Two:
    UNDERSTANDING FOOD..PAGE 24
    THE PROCESS OF HOW THINGS HAPPEN............................PAGE 26

Chapter Three:
    CRAFTING A CUISINE..PAGE 32
    FUTURE IDEALS..PAGE 36
    DIFFERENCES ARE DISTINCT..PAGE 38
    BUILDING A VIBE..PAGE 42
    WHAT IF DELICIOUS WAS EASY.......................................PAGE 52
    YOUR VOICE, YOUR IDEALS...PAGE 56

Chapter Four:
    FLAVORS...PAGE 64

Chapter Five:
    CHEFS AND FOODIES..PAGE 86
    THE PLAYERS...PAGE 89
        ALPHA CONTEMPORARIES.................................PAGE 90
        THE NOUVEAU GENERATION.............................PAGE 93
        THE THIRD GENERATION.................................PAGE 103

Chapter Six:
    YOUR FUTURE, SOCIAL MEDIA AND THE INTERNET.............PAGE 115
INDEX...PAGE 135

CHAPTER ONE:
CULTURE OF CUISINE:

BRINGING A TALENT TO BEAR DEVELOPS SOMETHING UNIQUE!

BREAKING IT DOWN INTO THE MOST ELEMENTAL LEVELS: *"CULTURE"* IS *CULINARY THOUGHT*…AND AS INNOVATION FORMS, IT BECOMES YOUR RELENTLESS COOKERY FORMULA. AS A CHEF, YOUR TASTE BUDS HAVE TO BE A GUIDE TO CORRECTNESS.

A COMMUNITY'S "CULTURE" IS A STAGE WHERE YOUR "CUISINE" IS THE LIMELIGHT, WHICH ACCENTUATES YOUR IDEALS AND THEORIES.

CULTURE OF CUISINE....

....BY SWEAT AND SOMETIMES TEARS.

OUR CULTURE OF CUISINE IS THE ACHIEVABLE ARTISTIC INVENTION AND MANIPULATION OF FOODS INTO A VALUED COMMODITY. IT IS REALIZED BY THE CONSUMER AS CUISINE, FORGED UNIQUELY THROUGH YOUR EXTRAORDINARY PROSPECTIVE AND INDIVIDUAL PORTRAYALS OF TASTE VARIANCES.

THE PROCESS OF THIS CULTURE IS SIMPLY DEVELOPING HOW A CHEF DEEMS IS THE BEST WAY TO PREPARE A FOOD COMMODITY INTO A STRUCTURED SUCCESSION ON THE PLATE.

ONE OF THE CHEFS I INTERVIEWED THINKS THAT RECIPES ARE LIKE YOUR CHILDREN. YOU HAVE TO GUIDE AND SHAPE THEM FOR THEIR TOTAL LIFE SPAN. IT IS THIS GUIDANCE THAT STRUCTURES A CHEF AS AN IDEALISTIC, CONCEPT CURATOR AND NOT JUST AN OBSEQUIOUS WORKER.

CHEFS REFLECT THAT CULTURE OF CUISINE IS A HEARTFELT ENTITY UNTO ITSELF THAT SPINS INTO A LIFELONG REPRESENTATION OF THEIR LIFE'S DISCIPLINE.

ALTHOUGH CUISINE STYLING CHANGES AS YOU TRAVEL ACROSS THIS AREA OF SOUTH FLORIDA, THERE IS A RESPECTIVE TREND THAT CHEFS FOLLOW. HEALTHY SEAFOOD CHOICES AND LOCALLY UTILIZED HARVESTS INCREASE IN DINING VENUES AS MENU POPULARITY INCREASES.

A MAJORITY OF OUR CUSTOMERS COME FROM SOMEWHERE ELSE. WHILE THEY ARE HERE, THEY WANT TO DINE ON THE BEST LOCAL EXAMPLES OF TYPICAL CULINARY ORDINATION.

FLORIDA HAS OVER 1000 MILES OF SHORELINE SO, SEAFOOD, OF COURSE, BECOMES A MAJOR PORTION OF OUR MENUS.

WE NATURALLY ALL STARTED COOKING LIKE OUR PREDECESSORS, WITH HEAVY CREAM AND BUTTER TO ENRICH A DISH'S TASTE.

NOW, A PLETHORA OF FRESH HERBS, OLIVE OIL, TROPICAL FRUIT AND THE APPLICATION OF CAPSICUM'S SEARING HEAT HAVE REARRANGED OUR MODERN CULINARY THESIS. BEING SPONTANEOUS AND OPEN ENOUGH TO CUSTOMIZE YOUR COOKING FOR THOSE WHO HAVE GLUTEN, NUT OR DAIRY REQUIREMENTS ARE ALL A PART OF CULTURE ON TODAY'S MODERN MENU.

HOW WAS OUR CUISINE CRAFTED?

~A STEP BACKWARD TO ENVISION AN EMERGING TREND.

FOODS ALONE DO NOT REPRESENT SOUTH FLORIDA'S CUISINE. IT IS THE SIGNIFICANCE AND FOOD-LOGY SURROUNDING THE ELEMENTARY SEA-BASED AND TROPICAL HARVESTS, ITS HERITAGE OF PREPARATION, THE COMBINATION OF SIMILAR FLAVORS; THE WHEN, WHERE AND WITH WHOM OF DINING, THAT DETERMINES THE *CULTURE* OF OUR CUISINE.

CUISINE IS WHAT MOST OFTEN SETS ONE CULTURE APART FROM ANOTHER. EVER SINCE THE FIRST COOKBOOK WAS PUBLISHED IN AMERICA - "AMERICAN COOKERY" PRINTED IN 1796 - AMERICAN FOODIES AND CHEFS HAVE BEEN DEFINING AMERICA'S CUISINE. CUISINE UNITES A COMMUNITY (OR A COUNTRY) AND SEPARATES IT FROM OTHERS.

UNTIL THE 1980'S, CULINARY AUTHORITIES QUESTIONED WHETHER AMERICA HAD A CULINARY IDENTITY UNTO ITSELF. SINCE THEN, NOT ONLY IS THERE AN ACCEPTED AMERICAN CUISINE, IT HAS BEEN ORDAINED INTO A SIGNIFICANT AND SEGMENTAL REGIONAL CUISINE. OUR NEWLY LOCALIZED CUISINE HAS BEEN DEFINING AND REFINING ITSELF FOR DECADES AND HAS PRODUCED ACCOLADES FROM GLOBAL CULINARY SANCTIONING AUTHORITIES.

UNLIKE L.A., SAN FRANCISCO OR N.Y.C., FLORIDA HAS NEVER BEEN A WELL-RESPECTED STOPOVER ON THE U.S. HAUTE-SPOT

NOSHING CIRCUIT. FOR THE WORLDWIDE ACCEPTED AUTHORITY ON CUISINE AND EVALUATOR OF ITS CREATORS, THE MICHELIN GUIDE, FLORIDA WAS NEVER THOUGHT OF AS A PLACE WORTHY OF ANOTHER LOOK. SOUTH FLORIDIAN RESTAURANTS SERVED FROZEN FISH FROM THOUSANDS OF MILES AWAY, PRE-MADE AND FROZEN CRAB CAKES, BREADED SHRIMP AND FROZEN NORTHERN ATLANTIC WATERS WHITEFISH LIKE SOLE AND FLOUNDER WHICH WERE THE BASIS OF SOUTH FLORIDA MENU CHOICES JUST THREE DECADES AGO. MUCH HAS CHANGED SINCE 1980.

WE STARTED CHANGING IDEALS WITH CREDIBLE LOCAL FOODS. THERE WERE OUR KEY WEST STONE CRABS, LAKE OKEECHOBEE ALLIGATOR AND UBIQUITOUS KEY LIME PIE. SINCE THE MID-1990'S, OUR CUISINE HAD PREDOMINATED AMERICA'S HOTTEST NEW FOOD TRENDS WHERE FOOD LOVERS AND CRITICS CAME FROM ALL POINTS OF THE GLOBE TO SOUTHERN FLORIDA TO EXPERIENCE THE *NEW AND UNEXPECTED.* INSTEAD OF TEMPERATE AMERICAN REGIONAL FOODS LIKE MINI SQUASHES, FIDDLEHEAD FERNS AND SUN-DRIED TOMATOES, WE HAVE TURNED THE

> OUR PREVIOUS CULINARY CULTURE

DINER ONTO CILANTRO, MANGO AND SCOTCH BONNET PEPPER SEARED GULF OF MEXICO GROUPER, OR A WOOD-FIRE GRILLED FLORIDA POMPANO WITH CRUSHED PECANS AND CITRUS THAT IS SERVED WITH A *"COULIS-GRETTE"* OF MANGO OR PASSIONFRUIT.

OUR LOCALLY ESTABLISHED CUISINE HAS BEEN EARMARKED AS A DISTINCTIVE REGIONAL PHENOMENON AND ONE OF THE HOTTEST CULINARY TRENDS IN THE 1990'S

ODE TO FLORIDA
A CULINARY WASTELAND OR DREAMLAND ?

A FEW YEARS AGO MANY CHEFS WOULD NOT HAVE QUESTIONED WHICH PART OF THAT STATEMENT WAS TRUE BUT, SINCE THE 1990'S AND THE DEVELOPMENT OF OUR NEW AMERICAN REGIONAL CUISINE ~ NEW WORLD CUISINE~ FLORIDA WILL NO LONGER BE KNOWN ONLY FOR ORANGES, BIKINIS AND SUNSHINE.

ALONG THE VAST COCONUT TREE-LINED COASTLINE OF SOUTH FLORIDA, A CULINARY EVOLUTION HAS TAKEN PLACE. THIS NEW STYLE HAS CONSUMED AND SURPASSED ALL THE PREVIOUS STYLES THAT HAVE COME BEFORE IT.

AS THE SUN CRESTS OVER THE HORIZON, SOUTH BEACH (OR SOBE TO LOCALS) FLOURISHES. THE NEW AMERICAN RIVIERA AWAKENS ALREADY TEAMING WITH PEOPLE. SOME JUST LEAVING NIGHTCLUBS AND SUN WORSHIPERS ARE JUST NOW ARRIVING. THE PARROTS SQUAWK IN COCONUT PALMS AS A FILM CREW WHICH HAS BEEN ON LOCATION SINCE FOUR A.M. AWAITS ANOTHER PERFECT SUNRISE. AS THIS MORNING'S SUN RISES ON THE TEFLON CITY, IT BRINGS WITH IT THE EXUBERANCE OF A CRISP NEW BEGINNING, JUST AS FLORIDA'S NEW FUSION CUISINE BRINGS THE FRESHNESS OF AN EMERGING NEW CULINARY NATION. NEW WORLD CUISINE WAS DEVELOPED WITH EMPHASIS ON ENERGY. EACH NEW PLATE PRESENTATION EMPHASIZES A SPIRITED STYLE KNOWN ONLY TO A SOUTH FLORIDA CHEF.

MAINLY THIS NEW AMERICAN REGIONAL CUISINE WAS DEVELOPED WITH THE HELP OF SOUTH FLORIDA'S FIVE INDIGENOUS CULTURAL CULINARY HISTORIES.

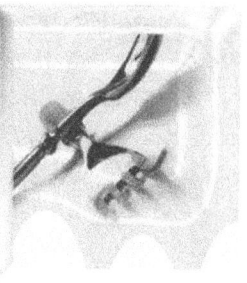

SOUTH FLORIDA'S EXOTIC COOKERY

THIS CULINARY PAST SETS A FRAMEWORK FOR OUR FUTURE. COOKING METHODS HAVE BEEN FUSED ALONG WITH CULINARY IDEOLOGIES. FURTHER, OUR RESIDENTS HAVE PLAYED A MAJOR PART IN THIS CUISINE'S DEVELOPMENT. NATIVE AMERICAN INDIANS, PEOPLE FROM THE OLD SOUTH, LATINOS, CARIBBEAN PEOPLES AND ASIANS HAVE ALL PLAYED A PART IN THIS FORMULATION. SOUTH FLORIDA CHEFS HAVE MELDED THESE COOKERY HERITAGES INTO A FUSION OF FOOD PREPARATION THAT HAS AMPLIFIED OUR DISPARATE MENU CREATIVITY.

ENTIRE PLATE PRESENTATIONS TYPICALLY HIGHLIGHT A LOCALLY PROCURED "SUPERSTAR" FOOD. SOME OF THESE "EXOTICA" SUPERSTAR FOOD EXAMPLES COULD BE: MAMAY, PAPAYA, LICHEE, LONGAN, STARFRUIT, UGLIFRUIT, ROLLINIA, ATEMOYA, RED BANANAS, CANISTEL, JACKFRUIT, SAPODILLA, NAME', BONIATO, CASSAVA, MALANGA, MANGO,

PLANTAIN, CHAYOTE, CALABAZA, PASSIONFRUIT, LOQUAT AND ACKEE.

AN EXAMPLE OF HOW THE COOKERY METHODOLOGIES HAVE BEEN MINGLED WOULD BE WHEN A CHEF GRILLS A (NATIVE-COOKING) YELLOWTAIL SNAPPER (LOCAL SEAFOOD SPECIES) AND SERVES WITH A SALSA (LATINO) OF MANGO AND SCOTCH BONNET PEPPER (CARIBBEAN). ALL OF THIS WOULD HAVE BEEN SPLATTERED WITH A "COULIS-GRETTE" (FUSION OF METHODOLOGIES) OF CANISTEL (CUBAN) AND ATEMOYA (A "SUGAR APPLE"~LOCAL EXOTIC FRUITS). THIS WOULD BE ACCOMPANIED BY A DUMPLING (OLD- SOUTHERN) OF MALANGA (CARIBBEAN FOOD PRODUCT) THAT HAS BEEN STEWED IN A LEMONGRASS (ASIAN) BROTH. IT IS THE ALLURE OF THESE EXOTIC FOODS THAT ADDS A TONGUE-TIED EXUBERANCE AND A HEIGHTENED METROPOLITAN OUTLOOK.

SECOND, THE *TASTE-VARIANCE* THAT OCCURS WHEN THESE LOCALLY HARVESTED TROPICAL FOODS ARE BLENDED, IS HARD TO REPLICATE ELSEWHERE IN THE UNITED STATES. IT IS OUR SUB-TROPICAL CLIMATE THAT MAKES IT POSSIBLE FOR US TO GROW EXOTIC TROPICAL PRODUCTS. BECAUSE THEY CANNOT TOLERATE FRIGID TEMPERATURES, MANY OF THESE TROPICAL FOODS ARE UNABLE TO GROW ELSEWHERE IN THE CONTINENTAL UNITED STATES. SO EVERY NEW PLATE BRINGS WITH IT A SCRUMPTIOUS FOOD COMBINATION THAT COULD NOT HAVE BEEN DEVELOPED ELSEWHERE IN THE UNITED STATES.

OF COURSE, SOUTH FLORIDA HAS A COASTAL BOUNTY THAT IS HARD TO MATCH. THE SHEAR ABUNDANCE OF SEAFOOD ITEMS IS STAGGERING. THERE ARE: ATLANTIC SWORDFISH, DOLPHINFISH (MAHI-MAHI), JACKS, KINGFISH, MACKERELS, TUNA, YELLOWTAIL SNAPPER, WAHOO, FOUR DIFFERENT LOCALLY CAUGHT SNAPPERS AND FIVE DIFFERENT GROUPERS, POMPANO, STONE CRAB, CLAMS, LOBSTERS, ROCK SHRIMP, CONCH, (WHITE, PINK, GREEN AND BROWN) SHRIMP, SCALLOPS, OYSTERS, ETC... THE LIST IS QUITE LENGTHY AND GETTING LONGER ALL THE TIME.

BESIDES THESE ITEMS THE *INLAND AND FARM RAISED* FOOD PRODUCTS ARE BECOMING MORE POPULAR EVERY DAY. FLORIDA ALSO HAS A SPECIALITY GROUP OF HARVESTERS LIKE THE SEMINOLE INDIANS, THAT PROVIDE PRODUCTS SUCH AS: VENISON, WILD TURKEY AND BOAR, HARE, QUAIL, ALLIGATOR, FROG LEGS, BASS, STRIPED BASS, PERCH, CRAYFISH, TROUT, CATFISH AND EVEN HEART OF PALM (A.K.A. SWAMP CABBAGE).

THIS MELDING OF EXOTIC AND THE COMMONPLACE HAS MADE CULINARY *SUPERSTARS* OUT OF OUR LOCALLY-HARVESTED EXOTIC PROVISIONS. JUST AS FRANCE HAS BEEN KNOWN FOR ITS SPECIALIZED REGIONS (IE...LYONS, BURGUNDY, ETC...) SO WILL SOUTH FLORIDA WHEN IT COMES TO AMERICAN REGIONAL CUISINE.

Chapter Two

Understanding Food...

Understanding the Relationships of Ingredients

The Destiny of Ingredients

Using the magic food combo of scallion, ginger and garlic is the Asian culinary equivalent to the French classic "Mirepoix".

South Florida chefs always believe that some ingredients should be paired together...

Other times the destiny of ingredients is to be prepared simply so the diner can enjoy the essential food element alone.

Some chefs believe in a holy trinity of garlic, tomato and basil and sure, they make a naturally great tasting combination but, there is so much more. Look at salsa combinations. Where tomatoes or substitute any other flavorful ingredient like mango or papaya, are paired with the basic combination of jalapeño, lime juice, onions and cilantro.

In the Latino-based cuisines of the Caribbean, there is sofrito. It takes the perfect combination of onion, garlic, peppers and stews them together to form a paste that goes into soups and sauces as well as being used as a marinade.

THE POINT BEING, MANY OUTWARDLY NATURAL OCCURRING FOOD COMBINATIONS COMPLEMENT EACH OTHER. YOU HAVE TO FIND THAT SPECIAL COMBINATION THAT MAKES YOU GLAD YOU BECAME A CHEF AND MAKE IT YOUR COOKERY SIGNATURE.

LET YOUR COOKERY IDEALS GUIDE YOU TO YOUR OWN DESTINY, FINDING YOUR WAY THROUGH YEARS OF HAPHAZARD CULINARY DAYDREAMING AND RECIPE FLUX. BEND WITH THE WINDS OF CULINARY CHANGE AND MAKE THE CURRENT TREND OF THE "TIMES" YOUR REASONING FOR NEW EXPERIMENTATIONS WITH YOUR OWN CULINARY IDEALS. WHEN THE CHANGES IN THE US DIET LOOKED TOWARDS HEALTHIER COOKERY OPTIONS, MANY CHEFS CHANGED. WHEN A NATIONAL EMPHASIS WAS ON HOW CHEFS SHOULD APPLY LOCALLY HARVESTED FOODS, CHANGES APPEARED ONCE AGAIN TO OUR MENUS. WHEN THE NEXT INNOVATIVE AND REAL THESIS ABOUT COOKING APPEARS ON THE NEW AMERICAN COOKERY SCENE, THEN WE SHOULD ALL EVALUATE AND CHANGE ALONG WITH IT.

THE LINE BETWEEN ART AND SCIENCE...

.....IS FADING. WITH THE ADVENT OF THE MODERN FAMILY AND THE WAY IT SHOPS FOR GROCERIES, THEY WILL FIND THE SHELVES ARE ALWAYS FULL OF FOODS PRESERVED AND FLAVORED WITH CHEMICAL ENHANCEMENTS. JUST READ THE LABELS. YOU WILL SEE THERE IS SCIENCE IN EVERY BOTTLE AND ON EVERY PACKAGE LABEL.

NATURALLY RAISED AND LOCALLY SOURCED PRODUCT IS THE WAY OF THE FUTURE. ALL CHEFS SHOULD TRY TO FIND THE BEST OF PRODUCTS FOR THEIR MENUS. GETTING IT LOCALLY SOURCED, ONLY HOURS OUT OF THE EARTH IS THE WAY RESTAURANTS ALWAYS DID IT IN FRANCE USING THE BEST, FRESHEST OF SEASON PRODUCTS FOR A MENU. THIS TREND IS NOW ALL THE RAGE BUT, HAD IT REALLY EVER HALTED? YOU CAN ALWAYS FIND THE VERY BEST RESTAURANTS USING THIS STYLE OF MENU CONCEPTION. IT IS NOW POPULAR TO FIND LOCAL FARMERS WILLING TO FARM CLOSER TO TOWNS AND URBAN CENTRES. OR IS IT THAT THE FARMERS ARE GETTING PAID MORE FAIRLY FOR A GENUINELY

BETTER PRODUCT? I THINK THE LATTER. PEOPLE THAT RAISE FOODS IN SOUTH FLORIDA HAVE EXPERIENCED A BLOSSOMING COST OF DOING BUSINESS. TODAY, CHEFS ARE NOW MORE WILLING TO PAY THE PREMIUM FOR A SUPERIOR PRODUCT BECAUSE THEIR REPUTATIONS HAVE BEEN BUILT ON SERVING ONLY THE BEST.

> IDEAS BEGET IDEALS

FOOD IS ART

ART IS THE DISCUSSION OF VALUE ADDED TO THE PLATE THROUGH GARNISHMENTS. THE MORE "ART" THERE IS IN THE PRESENTATION, THE MORE VALUE THE CUSTOMER PERCEIVES TO HAVE RECEIVED.

IDEALS... *MAKE THEM YOURS.* **EXECUTE YOUR** *VISION.*

TAKE YOUR THOUGHTS AND WRITE THEM DOWN. IF YOU DO NOT, AN ENLIVENING NEW CONCEPT WILL SLIP AWAY. ALWAYS KEEP A NOTEPAD WITH YOU. DEFINE THE SIMPLE ASPECTS OF A NEW IDEA, IDENTIFY AND REFINE THE PRIMARY FLAVORS. MAKE IT DISTINCTIVELY INDIVIDUALISTIC BY TWEAKING THE INGREDIENTS TO REFLECT YOUR OWN PALATE. AFTER YOU LIKE IT, GIVE IT TO OTHERS TO TRY AND SEE IF A WIDE RANGE OF PEOPLE LIKE IT. IF YOU DO NOT GET OTHERS TO COMMENT ON IT, THEN THE OLD ADAGE WILL HOLD TRUE - "ONLY SELL WHAT YOU LIKE AND YOU WILL FIND YOURSELF AS YOUR ONLY CUSTOMER."

THE PROCESS OF HOW THINGS HAPPEN

THE IMPORTANCE OF THE WRITTEN WORD WILL BECOME EVIDENT TO YOU SOON!

PRINT OUT YOUR BRAIN...

THINK, WRITE AND CREATE.

If your pose isn't clear and concise, people will not take your advice no matter its correctness. Writing recipes for cookbooks is different these days. There is so much diversity in what people want and what they can grasp. In the past, a woman that has just entered into a marriage usually wanted a *basic* cookbook to use in preparing simple, hearty meals for her new husband. Currently chefs everywhere have to produce recipes for the modern television cooking show viewer. Because of viewing TV cooking shows, your readers will now be more on top the "au courant" foods than the homemaker of the 60's and 70's.

Make it unique and memorable in the way you describe the recipe's most noteworthy highlights.

You should start by singing the praises of why anyone should try this recipe.

Writing is a communicative art. Use words to paint a picture of how to complete a recipe and give the reader a sense of what the finished dish should look like. Maybe you can start by telling a story about how a recipe was stumbled upon by mixing cookery ideals and methodologies. This is how Chef Norman Van Aken came to formulate the audacious and exotic genus of *New World Cuisine*.

The genesis of a *New World Cuisine* recipe is to take a lesser-known tropical fruit, grown in the Caribbean basin regions of the world, describe it in detail in the recipe heading, to ease into using the unfamiliar. Then, using universal cooking methods and techniques from Latin America, prepare this unfamiliar food element with a metropolitan plating style and Viola! He has walked you through a new wave recipe that you might have earlier thought was too nouveau for you to consider completing.

27

One Moment Please....

Your ideals and your unique culinary talents define you as a chef.

IDEALS DEFINE YOU

It is vital that you can and, are able to highlight your ideals by underscoring your talents to your patrons through written communications. Your ideals and your unique culinary talents define you. You have to make sure that others recognize these defining distinctions.

First, you want to partner with a communications specialist. You have to invest time to research who you are partnering with to distribute your communications. Then research who will publish your communications (magazines, websites, etc...) and who they have as readers. Get to know these information hawkers by reading their previously published articles. How have these articles helped the restaurant that they wrote about?

Compare the press release that generated enough interest from the article publisher to actually get printed. I have done this by getting on to a noted Press Agent's mailing list. You can learn how and why they write their content by reading their published *press release generated* articles. Learn how they structured the press release and what information was in the press release that was printed and, replicate this process yourself. After learning this formula and with a little practice, you should start to tell others about what you have accomplished through your press releases.

What has previously happened in our business when you submit information would only be used by a publisher if they needed the information for

A SPECIFIC PRE-PLANNED ARTICLE. WHAT WOULD BE BETTER FOR YOU WOULD BE TO GENERATE INTEREST IN SOMETHING YOU PLAN TO DO THROUGH PRESS RELEASES AND THEN HAVE THEM FOLLOW UP WITH YOU BEFORE THE EVENT OCCURS.

ATTRACT THE MEDIA'S ATTENTION BY GENERATING PRESS REFERRALS BACK TO YOU AS AN EXPERT IN YOUR CHOSEN SUBJECT. VAUNT YOURSELF AS AN EXPERT FOR THIS SUBJECT WHERE YOU CAN SHOW DEMONSTRATE A COMMANDING PANACHE OR STEWARDSHIP.

THIS ENTIRE PROCESS TAKES TIME BUT IT IS IMPORTANT TO ACCOMPLISH DURING YOUR ENTIRE CAREER.

YOU SHOULD THINK ABOUT IT LIKE THIS. IF THE TREE FALLS IN THE FOREST, AND THERE IS NO ONE THERE TO HEAR IT, DOES IT MAKE A NOISE? YOU CAN BE THE GREATEST CHEF, COOKING WITH THE MOST INNOVATIVE RECIPES BUT, IF YOUR FUTURE CUSTOMERS DON'T KNOW ABOUT IT, NO ONE BENEFITS. AND, YOU AREN'T RECOGNIZED FOR YOUR EXTRA-ORDINARY TALENTS.

MAKE YOUR IDEAS AND YOUR TALENTS UNDERSTOOD AND BE EMPOWERED BY THEM BY INFORMING OTHERS WHAT YOU DO WELL.

THIS IS A GOOD TIME TO LEARN HOW TO "*SEED*" THE 'NET. SEEDING IS POSTING PRESS RELEASES ON VARIOUS INTERNET SEARCH ENGINES. WHAT LEADS TO SUCCESS IS TO DEMONSTRATE YOUR ABILITY TO CREATE AND POST INTERESTING TOPICS THAT OTHERS WILL RE-PUBLISH. PUBLISHING IS EASY, JUST *GOOGLE:* **FREE PRESS RELEASE** AND, GO TO THE FORMS AND FILL OUT YOUR CONTACT INFORMATION AND START POSTING.

WHEN YOU HIT A CHORD WITH ANY MEDIA PUBLICATION, AND THEY PUBLISH YOUR INFORMATION, THEN RECREATE AND RESTRUCTURE THE CONTENT FOR YOUR NEXT MEDIA GOAL IN CONCURRENCE WITH THEIR CONTENT NEEDS AND DESIRES.

HAVING YOUR PRESS AS YOUR MOUTHPIECE YOU WILL CREATE AND QUANTIFY AN ATMOSPHERE OF QUALITY AT THE SAME TIME ESTABLISHING THE ACTUALITY THAT YOU AND YOUR IDEALS *ARE* WHAT DRIVE THE SUCCESS OF THIS

RESTAURANT. BRINGING RECOGNITION TO YOURSELF MIGHT SEEM TO MANY PEOPLE AS SELF-SERVING BUT, IN CASE AFTER CASE, THE CHEFS THAT I KNOW HAVE SECURED THEIR FUTURES BY BECOMING A "*FAMOUS*" CHEF. I KNOW CHEFS THAT HAVE PARTNERED WITH GREAT PR PEOPLE JUST TO MAKE SURE THEIR CULINARY FAME IS SECURED BECAUSE, THE MORE THE PR PERSON WORKS TO PUBLICIZE THE RESTAURANT THE MORE POPULAR THE CHEF BECOMES. WITH MANAGEMENT'S BACKING AND THEIR EFFORTS, BECOMING WELL-KNOWN IS EASILY REALIZED. EVERY NEW HERALDED CREDENTIAL, BOOSTS THE COMMUNITY'S RECOGNITION OF A RESTAURANT THAT IS MANNED BY AN ADMIRED CULINARY LEADER.

CLEAR AND DISTINCT VOICE

IF YOUR RESTAURANT'S COOKERY STANDARDS ARE BASED UPON DECADES OR EVEN CENTURIES OF CUISINE, YOU MENU HAS A DISTINCT CULINARY VOICE.

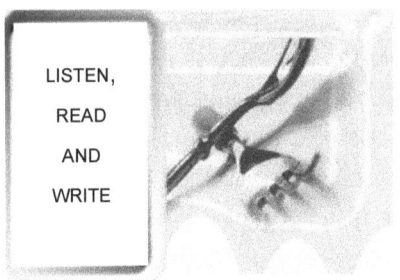

LISTEN, READ AND WRITE

THE MORE YOU EXPLAIN THINGS...

....THE MORE PEOPLE CAN UNDERSTAND WHAT YOU ARE TRY TO ACHIEVE. AND, WHY YOU ARE DOING THEM IN YOUR CHOSEN MANNER.

BE CLEAR AND GIVE REASONS WHY YOU HAVE PROCEEDED IN THE MANNER IN WHICH YOU ARE TRYING TO TEACH THEM. INSTRUCT THE LISTENER WITH AN APPRAISED LEVEL OF EXPERIENCE APPROACH. KNOW WHO YOUR LISTENERS ARE AND WHAT THEIR LEVEL OF EXPERIENCE IS BEFORE YOU START COMMUNICATIONS. GROOM THE INFORMATION TO THE RELEVANT SKILL OF THE LISTENER. TELLING SOMEONE TO USE A MIREPOIX WITHOUT THEIR KNOWING WHAT A MIREPOIX IS, WILL NOT HELP IN THIS EDIFICATION PROCESS.

THIS IDEAL AND PROCESS IS AS IMPORTANT AS ANY OTHER INFORMATION THAT YOU WILL LEARN FROM READING THIS BOOK.

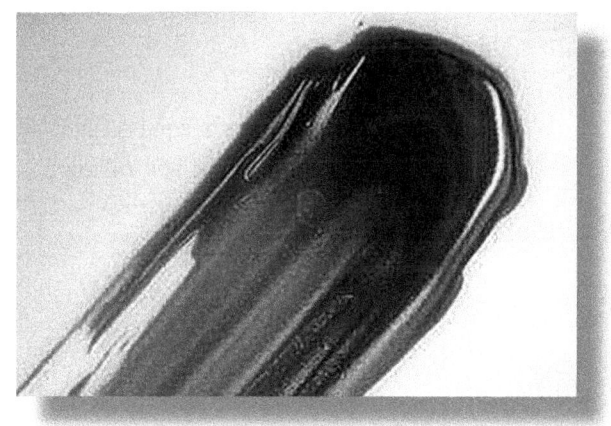

CHAPTER 3

CRAFTING A CUISINE

*LIKE-MINDED THOUGHTS BRING FORTH
A COMMON CULTURE.*

*THE FIRST THREE STEPS...
~LISTEN, READ AND CREATE~*

*THE BONDING OF CHEFS THROUGH
CUISINE IS UNENDING.*

"ARTISTS WILL BE ARTISTS" – NO MATTER THE MEDIUM. I HAVE FOUND THAT IF CHEFS WERE NOT CREATING ART WITH FOOD, THEY MOST LIKELY WOULD BE CREATING ART IN OTHER MEDIUMS.

PEOPLE THAT BECOME CHEF ARTISTS ARE OF A COMMUNITY WHO ARE SEARCHING FOR A WAY WHERE THEIR CREATIVE SIDE IS ABLE TO EXPAND AND, THEY SEEMINGLY ALWAYS WANT TO SATISFY OTHERS THROUGH THE ENJOYMENT OF THEIR PERSONALIZED AND SPECIFICALLY HONED COOKERY TALENTS.

SOME BECOME CHEFS ARTISTS FOR CELEBRITY WHILE
MOST THAT I KNOW DO IT FOR THE LOVE
OF ENRICHMENT OF ANOTHER.

As any chef will tell you, "This is the hardest job that I ever loved." For most chefs that I have met, this is true. Culinarians are a special bred of people.

Being a chef is about accepting something that people outside this realm will never know....

- It is the turmoil - that drives us.
- It is the heat and the frustration - that recharges us.
- It is always the daunting expectations - that drive us to perfection.
- It is the lack of surrounding culture - that makes us want to slice, weave and tie together works of edible art.
- It is the lack of ability - that make us want to educate further.
- It is the infinite - that drives us to calculated singularism.

Back to the Future?

Miami is a sand-laced, sun-drenched epicurean emporium that foodie gurus from around the world adore. It has been the birthplace of the most innovative American cuisine and our culinary vibe is a reflection of the city's multicultural identity.

Before moving the dialogue forward we have to look back a couple decades. South Florida based nouveau cuisine has had many poetic culinary labels like: New World, Floribbean, Tropical Fusion and Nuevo Latino. Whatever the tag, South Florida chefs have won national recognition and applause with their culinary representations of cuisine ideals.

Boasting the use of the freshest of locally harvested Florida seafood, adding in our unique tropical exoticness from fruits like: mango, sour sop, atemoya, papaya, passionfruit and, of course, a mélange of root vegetables like: boniato, malanga, yucca and taro,

OUR CULINARY THESIS HAS FAR ECLIPSED THE WOEBEGONE BLACKENED EVERYTHING AMERICAN CUISINE THAT EMERGED FROM LOUISIANA IN THE 1970'S. IT HAS FAR SURPASSED THE EARLY '80S GOURMET PIZZA AND ASIAN-BASED CALIFORNIA GEWGAW THEORY OF THE LATE 1980'S.

OUR CHEFS, WITH THEIR HABIT OF CULINARY RULE BREAKAGE AND INDULGING IN FANTASIES OF CULINARY WIZARDRY, HELPED AFFIRM THAT MIAMI-BASED CHEFS ARE AMONG OUR NATION'S MOST INNOVATIVE. OUR CULINARY THESIS IS EXCEEDINGLY DEPENDENT ON AN UNDER-REPRESENTED WEALTH OF A LOCALLY AVAILABLE TROPICAL FABRIC THAT ARE LOW IN FATS AND HIGH IN PAN-TROPICAL EXOTIC FLAVORS. THIS CUISINE WAS AMERICA'S SHOWCASE IN THE MID-1990'S.

OUR NEW CUISINE BOASTED USE OF HEALTHY EXOTIC FRUITS, VEGETABLES, SEAFOOD AND SPICES THAT ARE INDIGENOUS TO THE COUNTRIES FROM ALL ACROSS THE TROPICAL LATITUDES OF THE WORLD. THE BINDING ELEMENT TO THIS THESIS WAS THAT SOUTH FLORIDA IS SUB-

CREATIVITY AND SOUTH FLORIDA CHEFS

TROPICAL. IT IS THE ONLY PLACE IN THE CONTINENTAL UNITED STATES THAT CAN GROW THESE FOODS YEAR-ROUND.

THIS NEOCLASSIC CONCEPTUAL-IZING EMANATES FROM SOUTH FLORIDA CHEFS AND IS STILL SEEN LARGELY IN OUR SEAFOOD-BASED MENUS. LOCALLY HARVESTED CLAMS, YELLOWFIN TUNA AND POMPANO FROM THE ATLANTIC, INDIAN RIVER BLUE CRAB, GULF OF MEXICO SHRIMP, SNAPPERS, DOLPHINFISH, GROUPERS AND LESSER-KNOWN MERIDIAN DELICACIES LIKE WAHOO AND COBIA ARE ALL A PART OF FLORIDA'S HISTORY OF FLAVORFUL OCEAN-BASED HARVESTS. IN THE SNAPPER FAMILY THERE ARE: YELLOWTAIL, MANGROVE, SILVER, HOG AND MUTTON -- ALL OF THEM SWEETER AND MORE TENDER THAN THE ATLANTIC RED SNAPPER THAT IS SHIPPED OUT OF STATE TO MOST EVERYONE ELSE IN OUR COUNTRY.

Grilling over Florida hard woods (oak), influenced by ancient Caribbean cookery techniques is an indispensable healthier cookery practice. As South Florida continues to be a bain marie for the Caribbean, Central and South American cultures, our cuisine is constantly being influenced and altered by the culinary styling of ideals from nations such as: St. Maarten, Dominican Republic, Cuba, Jamaica, Chile, Mexico, Peru, Argentina and Brazil.

> "The destiny of nations depends on the manner in which they are fed."
> —Jean-Anthelme Brillat-Savarin (1825)

The mis en place of salsas, mojos, mops, rubs and adobo seasoning concoctions - that are nourished by locally harvested flora - are vital flavoring ingredients that have helped set us apart for decades. Our culinary posture mulls over the thought that chefs who were trained in the "Old World" classic cookery methodologies, continue to forge healthier dining presentations with a plethora of "New World" ingredients that boast a yet unseen cookery conceptions on South Floridian menus.

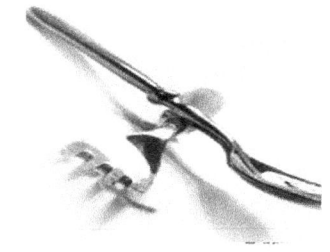

Sustenance to our chef's future ideals...

Something new and different has happened in South Florida. A culinary movement was started and is still vibrant here three decades later. South Florida's citizenry has a strong sense and allegiance to where they come from and it is illustrated daily in so many artistic ways.

Many contrasting cultures live in South Florida. Many share a communal ancestry. World-wide, cuisine acts as a mirror of a culture, just as dance or works of art. Cuisine also provides a common understanding of what it means to "belong" to a particular dominion. James Beard said almost the same thing in 1982. Seen day in and day out in South Florida where similar cultures have menus using similar foods that are characteristically prepared in polar directions.

The region in which the cuisine developed might have a regional-based namesake. Their names give all further culinary conceptions a sense of meaningful posture in its locale and its worldly perception. This is how the terms "New World Cuisine" and "Caribb-ican" have come into our South Florida culinary vocabulary. These terms are used to denote the types of food or a structure of culinary preparation and it helps the diner understand the chef's culinary ideal.

CONSEQUENTLY, THE *CULTURE OF OUR CUISINE* IS STRONGLY SLANTED IN THE DIRECTION OF A LATINO POINT OF VIEW. WHAT SETS A CULTURE APART ALSO GIVES UNITY TO OUR KINDRED COOKERY HERITAGES.

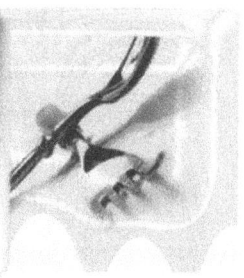

SO MANY OF TODAY'S TECHNIQUES WERE BUILT IN THE PAST.

WHETHER IT IS THE WEATHER....

IF A CULTURE IS DEFINED BY WHAT IS EATEN, HOW IT IS EATEN AND THE TIME OF DAY THEY CONSUME IT, THEN SOUTH FLORIDA IS A CENTRAL AMERICAN ASSEMBLAGE OF CULINARY THOUGHTS AND IDEALS. OUR FUTURE CULINARY DIRECTION COMES FROM THESE HERITAGE-INFLUENCED POSTURES.

FOR DECADES, PEOPLE IN SOUTH FLORIDA DINED LATER IN THE DAY. THE WEATHER IS WARM SOME MIGHT SAY IT IS HOT MOST OF THE YEAR. PEOPLE LIKE TO DINE LATER IN THE EVENING WHEN IT IS COOLER. MANY CULTURES FROM EQUATORIAL REGIONS OF THE WORLD DO THE SAME. THEY DINE LATER IN THE EVENING BECAUSE OF THE EQUATORIAL WARMTH OF THEIR HOMELAND.

WARM WEATHER HAS HAD A LOT TO DO WITH WHAT HAS BECOME POPULAR ON MENUS IN SOUTH FLORIDA. BECAUSE OF THE WARMTH, OUR CUISINE IS LIGHTER IN ITS EVOLUTION THAN NORTHERN CULINARY TENDENCIES. OUTDOOR DINING ON PROMENADES LINED WITH COTTON CANDY TINGED BUILDINGS AND OUR WARM WEATHER ATTRIBUTES, VEER PEOPLE TO LIGHTER, HEALTHIER DINING. BECAUSE OUR CUISINE IS STOCKED FULL OF LIGHTER HEALTHY SALAD ENTREES, SOUTH FLORIDA'S COOKERY CONCEPT IS NATURALLY DIFFERENT.

DIFFERENCES ARE DISTINCT...
CHEFS WILL PREPARE A FOOD ITEM IN THE WAY THAT MOST SUITS HIS CHOSEN CULINARY IDEALS.

This style molds the thought process that we use as a guideline to perfecting a new menu's melodic theme. If the culture in the kitchen is one of innovation, the diner should be amazed at the unlimited adventures that can be written between the boundaries of a plate's rim. If the culture of the kitchen is one of perfection, then repetition of only one aspect in cookery categorization is expected.

In South Florida, chefs always use local foods. In the past few decades, tropically inspired lighter seafood menus have propagated. Our modern American culinary approach has charmed patrons to expect and demand these products, prepared in uncommon ways.

This is how it should be, no matter the locale of your restaurant. If you live in New York, you should make use of the local corn and vine grown veggies like squash, wild mushrooms, fiddlehead ferns, lobster and salmon. Wherever you are in the world, generating menus that reflect the area in which you live and work should be of utmost importance when developing your culinary ideals.

MASTERING THE MATERIALS:

Without replication, again and again, dozens and dozens of times, one cannot harmoniously and expertly duplicate a technical or physical process. This process is the stabilizing factor of Cuisine.

Artistically "Chef-like"

When all is said and done, Cuisine is a steadfast progression to perfection.

Look at the French Classical Cuisine. It has been perfected over hundreds of years, never changing, using the same ingredients prepared in the same manner, over and over again. This is a throttle that we do not use here in South Florida. French Classical teaching helps mold the basics of our cookery techniques yet, we expand and stretch its elements into something that is unique. Without the concrete footing of French Classical, "we would have to reinvent every dish over and over again", says chef Michael Bloise.

"Be quiet when the chef speaks and take plenty of notes." That is what I heard a lot when I was at C.I.A. during my formative years. You never know as much as you think you do. "Just listen and be ready to absorb as much as you can within your short time here", says my chef instructor. "Even if you are completely confident in your new abilities after graduation, if you don't learn something new every day when you are in your new position, leave and find a place where you can. Then when you think you do know everything, look to the Chinese, they have been cooking for 5,000 years," he continues.

There is something to be said about time. It takes time to learn. It takes time to evaluate. It takes time to formulate your own ideals.

Mastering a culinary thesis - that you believe in - takes time to replicate and time to perfect. Being the one who has to take taught ideals and pass it on to others also takes time. It takes time for others to acquire the knowledge and for them to absorb it and endorse your teachings as it soaks into their own psyche. So mastering a cuisine is all about time.

Cultivating Ideas:

For the budding chefs of tomorrow there is the internet and smart phone technologies. How easy is it now to cross the culinary universe with the flick of a switch? You will find yourself researching and extracting information from uncommon places to formulate your seamless culinary position. Always being curious is how I have pushed myself to do greater things in my field.

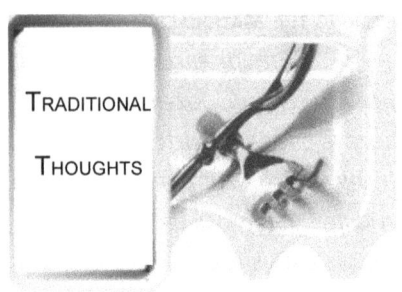

Traditional Thoughts

Always say to yourself.. "is good enough, ever enough"? There should never be a time when you are content with the status-quo.

Tomorrow's culinary classics are yesterday's future.

Using today's modern culinary styling will help you build tomorrow's culinary classics. Look at spa cuisine and the healthy California cuisine movement of the 1980's. It has reshaped today's American cookery. Being on the cusp of a culinary trend is the best way to better your game. Defining yourself as a leader of trends will boost your *need* to be better everyday. It is this elevated level of stress that keeps you grasping for more.

I find that a day at the ocean, maybe walking on South Beach or even the right tune on the radio helps me create. Daydreaming is always a necessary process for creation.

When I am in an atmosphere of Classical music, I find myself striving for "classical" perfection. While in the middle of the dinner rush, I always listen to my favourite *Trance* or ripping guitar licks from a 1980's Hair band. Walking the streets of South Beach, I find the architecture and the vibe from the throng strolling along the streets helps me to strive towards an expressive culinary spin out. Other times I explore the tropical fruit laddened back roads of the Redlands, to gain a feeling of exotic experimentation and innovation.

The how and the when of innovation seems to be polar among chefs but, you always need to be an ideal pioneer.

BUILDING A "VIBE"

Using the Internet's technical resources are time saving devices as well as a curse. The Internet's time saving and interconnect ability can also be your worst nightmare. One bad meal can be posted on the 'Net and follow you for an entire career.

The 'Net will also allow you to create an atmosphere of newness every day. You need to create a platform where new dishes, appended menus and recreated healthy dishes should be improvised daily so customers can see you intend to expand their dining experiences. Create a blog and use it in a daily delivery of your unique in-house happenings.

This will create the feeling of renewal and impulsive in-house happenings and it will draw your customers in to daily check to see what you are going to do next.

The more you change, the more opportunities you have the ability to draw their attention. It becomes easier to keep their continued interest as you become known for this change.

A certain portion of your clientele will want stability on the menu. That is when you use the Internet for sending out those reminders about how great their experience was last time they were there and, they should be continually reminded to come back to see more.

The Internet is your marketing tool that produces the best results quickly.

Many restaurants are so trendy the chefs set the vibe of "change" as its image. Being on the apex of a culinary trend can only last so long.

Who continues to boast they still cook in the style they did in the 1980's?

Look at these: blackened fish, gourmet pizzas, Southwestern or California cuisine and soon the molecular fad proves over time that it is just a fad! Always look for the change that leads to improvement. For example, as Spa Cuisine and California Cuisine helped turn America's eye towards healthy dining habits.

If you are known for changing menus, that is your vibe. Change just for change is not enhancement. Changes that advance a menu and continually draw people to your front door is an improvement.

People I have known in this business have done this for years without end. The technique is just as easy as the change. Keeping the

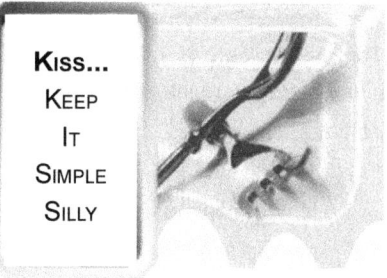

Kiss...
Keep
It
Simple
Silly

same protein on the plate, you just change its starch, veggie compliment, marinade or the sauce. The changes don't have to be dramatic, but they do have to be noticeable.

The *Scene* as the Vibe...
I found that a "vibe" can be the scene that takes place within your restaurant. Food, like fashion, is always trendy and ever changing. To be on the cusp of a changing culinary movement is just as important in the food business as it is to have your clothing designs displayed in New York City during fashion week if you were a clothing designer.

The restaurant's scene is extremely important on South Beach. Everyone wants to be in the place that is known as the "*scene*". It is the place where people

GO TO SEE AND BE SEEN. IT COULD BE THE LAST NAIL IN YOUR COFFIN IF YOU CAN'T GET THAT VIBE IN A SOUTH BEACH RESTAURANT.

IF YOU WORK IN A BREAKFAST PLACE, THEN THE *SCENE* SHOULD BE A PLACE BOASTING THIS IS THE BEST PLACE FOR LOCALS TO MEET. IF YOU WANT TO BUILD A SPECIAL VIBE AS A BREAKFAST PLACE, THEN YOU WILL HAVE TO MAINTAIN A FRIENDLY "LOCALS ARE THE MOST SPECIAL CUSTOMER" FEEL TO KEEP THE REGULARS COMING BACK. THAT IS WHERE THE INTERNET COMES IN HANDY. THROUGH EMAILS, BLURBS ON BLOGS, PHOTO POSTING AND LINKS, YOU CAN CREATE AN ONGOING VIBE THAT WILL BE EVER-CHANGING AND EVER-PRESENT.

WHAT IF THERE WERE NO TRADITIONS?

IF THERE WERE NO HERITAGE OF COOKERY TRADITIONS, WOULD YOU BE BUILDING SOMETHING LIKE CROSS-CULTURAL CUISINE EVERY TIME YOU COOK? CHEFS SAY THAT IF THERE WERE NO TRADITIONAL BASIS OF CUISINE, THE SAME THINGS WOULD HAVE TO BE INVENTED OVER AND OVER AGAIN. MOST PEOPLE IN MY GENERATION USE CLASSICAL

DEFINE YOUR IDEAS OF COOKERY

FRENCH CUISINE AS THEIR CULINARY GROUNDING. USING FRENCH CLASSICAL TO BASE EVERYTHING THAT THEY CONCEIVE FOR THE FUTURE IS THE GLUE THAT HOLDS US ALL TO A GAME PLAN.

THEN WE SHOULD ALSO LOOK AT "GLOBAL" CUISINE. IT IS AN IDEAL OF COOKERY THAT TAKES AN INGREDIENT FROM ONE CULTURE OR REGION OF THE WORLD AND PAIRS IT WITH OTHER DISSIMILAR INGREDIENTS OR COOKERY METHODS IN NONTRADITIONAL WAYS.

IN ONE KITCHEN I HAVE SEEN THREE GENERATIONS OF KITCHEN TRADITIONS IN PLAY AT ONCE. SOMETIMES IT IS THE CULTURE OF THE RESTAURANT THAT DRIVES ITS TRADITION. THE TRADITION CAN BE FORMULATED BY THE MIXTURE OF COOKERY HERITAGES. A GREAT EXAMPLE OF THIS IS THE CARIBBEAN RESTAURANT SCENE.

The reason is because the heritage of Caribbean cookery is one of intermixture. When the local Caribbean island people were being inhabited by the Europeans, the cookery traditions of the entire island changed. When the island was fought over by warring European economies and when the ruling class changed, the cuisine of the island changed. Not that everything was just forgotten, it was amended to the new faction's desires.

The traditions of the fledgling eatery, that might want change, is easier to change than their diminutive culinary heritage.

When a chef comes to an already running kitchen, he will find that if there is an extensive set tradition, he will have to incorporate the restaurant's established culinary history into his current cookery patterns.

Successful restaurants with long histories of culinary traditions are not going to want change. There has to be something dramatic such as a name change for the customers to accept menu change in traditions.

Exchanging Ideas and Ideals.
What better way to explore and define your "Cuisine" than to bounce ideas back and forth with like-minded peers. I always try to learn something new every day. I love going into a friend's kitchen and work a day alongside of him. I will watch how another chef creates something new or observe the way his staff interacts with each other. Their supplementary assiduous ideals will help your cookery thesis. When you are done implementing these new ideals, the final outcome in your kitchen has to be harmoniously balanced between what was and the newly ratified.

The exchanging of ideas is different than the inter-changing of ideals. Ideals have to be similar if an interchange of ideas is to be transferred on an equal culinary plane.

IDEALS HAVE TO BE COMMON BETWEEN PEERS OR YOU ARE NO LONGER A PEER, BUT THE STUDENT. COMMON AND EQUIVALENT IDEALS ARE WHAT WILL ASSEMBLE US AS AN EQUAL ORGANIZATION OF MEMBERS- NOT FOLLOWERS.

IDEALS ARE WHAT KEEP US HUNTING FOR MORE, STRIVING TO MAKE THE UNCOMMON MORE COMMONPLACE.

IDEAS HELP US GET THERE.

LEARNING AND CHANGING IDEAS INTO IDEALS FEEDS YOUR IMAGINATION. IMAGINATION IN TURN FEEDS THE CREATION PROCESS FOR YOUR NEXT BIG CULINARY DISCOVERY.

WEAKENED DESIGN

IT IS NOT THE IDEA OF THIS BOOK TO SAY YOU SHOULD MIMIC *TALENT TRAITS* AROUND YOU. IT IS TO REINFORCE THE IDEA THAT IT IS BETTER FOR YOU NOT TO WALK THROUGHOUT LIFE WITH BLINDERS ON...ONLY PERFORMING

DAILY RESPONSIBILITIES THAT ARE STAGNANT AND AGED.

WHILE WORKING AND LEARNING FROM OTHERS, YOU WILL GET THE OPPORTUNITY TO ADJUST A WAY OF PHILOSOPHY THAT YOU HAVE ALWAYS USED. WHY CAN'T YOU MAKE SAUCES WITHOUT THE USE OF A ROUX. FINDING ALTERNATIVES TO RECIPES WITH ADDED GLUTEN IS GOING TO BE AN IMPORTANT TRAIT CHEFS WILL HAVE TO MASTER FOR THE FUTURE. AS THE POPULARITY IN GLUTEN-FREE DINING GROWS, ALTERNATIVES TO THE WAY YOU WERE TAUGHT TO COOK WILL EMERGE. IT IS THIS CONSTANCY OF CHANGE THAT WILL MAKE YOU AN ALL AROUND CHEF.

WEAKENING A DESIGNED RECIPE IS NOT THE IDEA HERE EITHER. IT IS WITH CHANGE THAT WE GROW. DEEPENING THE MAGNITUDE OF CULINARY TRAITS AWARENESS IS the way that chefs can pursue this career for years. When recipes and previously known talents change it is not a weakening of your culinary traits, it is forging new ideals upon preceding structure of ideas.

Organize it: REPETITION makes it simple!

Repetition is commonplace in my kitchen. All of my fellow chefs have to learn cookery procedures as I see appropriate.

Repeating the procedure over and over and over is the way I train my people to do what I do.

Repetition, making it repeatedly, your cuisine is simplified by finding a better, more efficient path to correctness. It has always been the dozen little things you do perfectly everyday that makes it all work together.

Once you have mastered the singular step of finding a great taste, you can expand the process to intersperse the particular elements into an entire menu. Repetition of a dish and making it healthier, more cost efficient by removing wasted processing steps or being able to hold for longer periods, you have found common sense and timesaving cuts to get the best of both worlds.

After the tedious work is over, then the creative side of cooking will emerge.

Modify you Ideals.

My drive is always changing. My ideals don't change as much as my recipes do. Creation of new recipes brings to me the desire to make more recipes or even rework others to include new twists I didn't think about when they were created.

Forced to change your ideals always meets resistance. When it is necessary for survival of a business, it can be the most gratifying change of all. There is nothing better than to see your ideas succeed and when you measure the results.

WHEN VINDICATION FROM SUCCESSFUL RESHAPING OF IDEALS IS PROVEN, EVERYONE WINS. THIS IS WHAT DRIVES ME AND I AM SURE MANY OTHERS IN THIS *CULTURE OF CUISINE*.

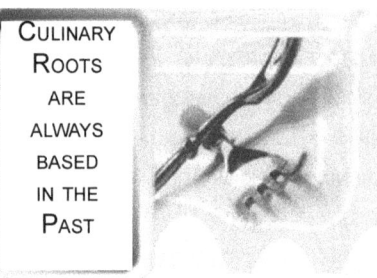

CULINARY ROOTS ARE ALWAYS BASED IN THE PAST

THE JOY OF SIMPLICITY...

AS YOU REPEAT PROCESSES, THE EASIER AND SIMPLER THEY BECOME.

THE IDEAL OF SIMPLE FOODS IS NOT THE SAME AS SIMPLISTIC FOODS. SIMPLISTIC RECIPES ARE BRIGHT WITH TASTE, NOT OVERWHELMED BY CREAM OR AN OVERLY BITTER REDUCED SAUCE. A FRESH FROM THE (LOCAL) FARM FRUIT MADE INTO A COULIS-GRETTE THAT IS LIGHTLY APPLIED TO A SIMPLE GRILLED, LOCALLY HARVESTED GROUPER IS THE WAY I HAVE BEEN COOKING FOR MANY YEARS. I ALWAYS TRY TO CREATE RECIPES THAT ARE SIMPLE, WITH BRIGHT INGREDIENTS UNCLUTTERED BY OVERPOWERING WINE REDUCTIONS OR FRENCH CLASSICAL CUISINE SANCTIONED ARTERY CLOGGING SAUCES.

USING LOCAL FOODS FOR BUILDING A SIMPLISTIC PREPARATION IS PARAMOUNT. LOCALLY AVAILABLE FOODS WILL ALWAYS BE FRESHER, BETTER IN QUALITY AND THIS WILL SHOW THROUGH IN YOUR FINAL DISH.

PREPLANNING A DISH MIGHT BE AS IMPORTANT AS USING THE FRESHEST INGREDIENTS. GETTING THE FRESHEST LOCAL INGREDIENTS IS SOMEWHAT HAPHAZARD. SOMETIMES YOU NEVER KNOW WHAT COMES IN FROM YOUR LOCAL GROWER. I HAVE ALWAYS HAD AN AGREEMENT WITH MY PURVEYORS THAT IF IT IS THE BEST, FRESHEST, LOCALLY AVAILABLE PRODUCT, THEN I WANT IT. SOMETIMES I GET BOXES FROM LOCAL GROWERS MARKED SPECIAL. THIS IS ESSENTIALLY MY MYSTERY BOX OF THE DAY. THIS SPONTANEOUS GIFT HEIGHTENS MY ENJOYMENT OF THIS BUSINESS.

When we all have to reach "outside the box" to do something a little different, that makes our daily challenges more enjoyable.

TEXTURE WILL DEFINE THE DISH

Soft and crunchy, light and rich, crisp and limp ~ all are Yin and Yang of cookery opposites. Cookery opposites directly affect one another and balance one another. Direct opposites balance a dish's mouthfeel, something interesting that tells the guests that thought was involved with the way the dish was conceived. In this way a chef has prepared a menu item that speaks for itself.

You have to let the ingredients speak their own language. The simpler the preparation, the easier the food speaks to the diner. Instead of adding flavor boasting spices that sometimes just overpower a dish, the chef should alternatively opt for using a simple grilling effect to boost the natural anomie that Mother Nature already injected into this dish, this is the direction you want to forge. The taste is only one part of your dish's perceived value. Textures and contrasts of soft or crispy, the way it affects the diner's gustatory experience, is a common tool in a chef's "cookery-ideal" toolbox. Hot and cold is one way to turn a diner on to a grilled chicken breast with a fresh salsa cru but, when it is a fruit salsa, you have brought in sweet, sour, cold, hot, rigid, limp, timid and sharp contrasting tastes, textures and multiple sensory judgments into a single *colourful* presentation.

COLOR AND LIGHT...

Color. Color. Color. You are working with a blank canvas.

You place foods on a white plate in a stylistic manner but, if there isn't a balance of colors on the plate as well, it won't have the same effect on the eye. Added artificial light in the dining environment also plays an important role of how the eye perceives color on your canvas.

49

Make use out of natural sunlight when you present food. When you are trying to photograph food this is even more important.

Natural light settings make natural things look right. The colorful balance of tomatoes and herbs jump out from the plate when you are dining outside. It is the natural light source that will enhance your food's brightness like no artificial light source can. Balance on the plate is important when remembering the first rule of thumb in dining, "customers eat with their eyes first".

The Uses of Light and Shade-

Everything tastes better when it looks good on the plate. "People eat with their eyes first" was something I heard every day when I was a novice chef.

The bright colors of a Capresse salad with the bursting red of tomato and vibrant green of the basil is a natural representation of the way colors occur in nature. When plate presentations mimic the way the food occurs naturally, it is a guaranteed hit for the eyes and starts delivering that ah-h-h feeling to your senses.

When I retouch photos of food in Photoshop (a computer program that can improve the quality of pictures), I always play with the food's tone. When you deal with the food's looks you have to have a strict defining line between light and dark so the picture reprints well in a cookbook. It is the same with your eyes. When natural light shines upon a natural product like food your senses are calmed. When unrealistic colors and tones are splashed in front of you the natural reaction is to wince.

The joy of simplicity can be in the way we perceive beautiful food. Stark contrasts don't always make for the best use of light and shade. If you are looking for dramatic changes in the plate's contrasts in shades of color, think pastels. As you add cream to sauces, the color turns

FROM STARK TO SHADOWY. THIS EYE-PLEASING INTERLUDE CAN LEAD INTO ANOTHER TASTE-VARIANCE ON THE PLATE OR CONTRAST IN ITS BITE.

STARK IS NOT ALWAYS SIMPLE BUT IT WILL DEFINE. THE BLUNTNESS IN THE CHANGING OF COLOR BALANCE ON THE PLATE SAYS TO YOUR MIND'S EYE, THERE IS SOMETHING NEW COMING. CHANGES IN THE SHADE BALANCE DO NOT MEAN CLEAN.

BALANCING THE SHADE ON YOUR PLATE, CALLS FOR UNDIFFERENTIATED STARKNESS BETWEEN EACH PREPARATION.

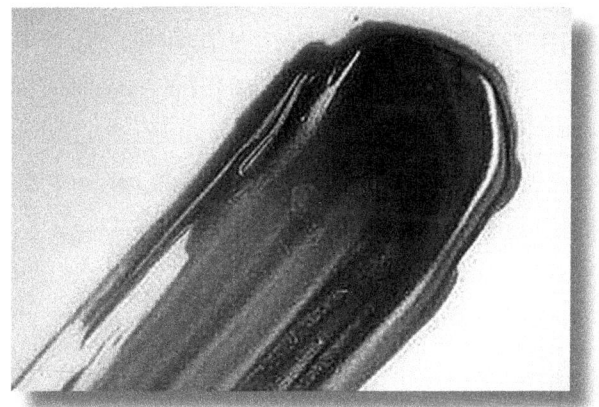

WHAT IF DELICIOUS WAS EASY?

IF DELICIOUS ENTREES WERE SIMPLE TO MAKE, EVERYONE WOULD HAVE THEIR OWN TELEVISION COOKING SHOW.

WE AS CULINARIANS CREATE VALUE THROUGH OTHER PEOPLE'S PERCEPTION.

CHEFS ARE TRYING TO BUILD VALUE IN PRESENTATIONS. IT IS THE VALUE THAT THE CUSTOMER SEES BEFORE THEY TASTE THE DISH THAT GIVES US THE ARTIST'S STYLE.

CHEFS DON'T WANT TO MOB A PLATE WITH TOO MANY BEAUTIFUL EDIBLES. USING THE "WHITE-SPACE" METHOD - WHICH IS POPULAR IN THE PRINT PUBLISHING INDUSTRY - A CHEF WANTS THE CUSTOMER SEE PLENTY OF CLEAN CANVAS (WHITE-SPACE) SO, PORTIONS HAVE TO BE SMALL.

IT IS THE BEAUTY OF THE FOOD ON A CLEAN CANVAS THAT ATTRACTS THE EYE AND THUSLY THE BRAIN SAYS "WOW, THIS MUST TASTE GOOD" BEFORE TAKING THE FIRST BITE. IT TAKES ME BACK TO MY MENTORS TELLING ME OVER AND OVER AGAIN; "IF THE CUSTOMER PERCEIVES THE BEAUTY FIRST WITH THEIR EYES, THE HEART WILL FOLLOW". IF YOU CAN GET THEIR HEARTS TO DEPEND ON YOUR COOKING STYLE, THEN YOU WILL HAVE A SUBSCRIBER FOR A LONG TIME.

If delicious were easy, anyone could put a piece of properly cooked seafood on a plate and you would have a single dinner sale. If you can get them to subscribe and relish your cookery styling, then you have a customer forever. It is never this easy. It is the balance of textures and tastes that make your creations art that can be enjoyed by all. It is the balance of shades of light and the simplicity of building a structured look to your plate that attracts a diner's attention. This takes years of soul searching as a chef, to cull out a cookery trend or element that works for him and abide by it. We know this is not for the novice. It is for the serious chef looking to fashion edible art for the soul.

Soul of the Food

Home cooked from Mom's kitchen is everyone's idea of getting back to the *soul* of cookery. Remembering the meals that grandma prepared with your mother in tow is the fondest of memories for any kindred remembrance. Being a part of those home cooked meals where family and sometime neighbours participated as a close-knit assemblage, made the holidays memorable for me. Family plays an important role in discovering your "soul" to food. Sometimes it is what we have learned at the apron strings of Mom or grandma that constitutes our future culinary ideals. The soul of your cookery probably comes from this upbringing as well.

Several chefs I have interviewed for this book follow this archetype. Raised on or near a farm, chefs love the idea of fresh out-of-the-soil food to use in their kitchens. It is a way of life that saturated many chef's professional careers. My mentors taught me the single best thing about living near the sea was experiencing the "soul" or the freshness of a freshly harvested fish. When I was a novice cook, Sushi was explained to me by an older Asian mentor. She thought that it was unnatural not to experience the freshness of a locally caught Black Grouper used in the style

THAT BEST SUITED IT – SUSHI! SHE INSTILLED THAT THE SOUL OF SUSHI IS THE GUISE THAT IT HAS TO BE THE FRESHEST POSSIBLE COMMODITY OR DON'T ATTEMPT IT.

Your writing will generate ideas.

CUISINE IS BASED UPON CENTURIES OF COOKERY HERITAGES

BASED UPON TRADITION, COOKERY HERITAGE IS WHAT HAS COME BEFORE IT, FORGED WITH INNOVATION. THE CHINESE POSSESS 5,000 YEARS OF CULINARY HISTORY BUT, OUR REGIONAL CUISINE SEEMINGLY AN INFANT WHEN IT COMES TO CULINARY HISTORIES, DOES HAVE A SURPRISING BIOGRAPHY. OUR *CARIBB*EAN - AMER*ICAN* (CARIBB-ICAN) COOKERY ROOTS HAVE BEEN CULTIVATED FOR CENTURIES. THE COOKERY HISTORIES OF SOUTH FLORIDA'S PAST ARE SHAPING OUR FUTURE CULINARY INHERITANCE. MANY OF THE MORE NOTABLE EATERIES IN SOUTH FLORIDA HAVE BASED THEIR MENU'S BIRTHRIGHT AFTER WHAT WE HAVE PREVIOUSLY CALLED "CARIBBEAN-FUSION" OR "FLORIBBEAN". NO MATTER THE NAMESAKE, CARIBB-ICAN CUISINE HAS A HISTORY OF CROSS-CULTURAL INNOVATION.

THE COOKERY HERITAGE OF SOUTH FLORIDA IS ONE OF AGGRESSIVE TROPICAL FRESHNESS WITH INTIMATIONS OF BOLDNESS. CHEFS MAKE IT A BENCHMARK TO NARRATE A PERSONAL COOKERY JOURNEY THROUGH THE MENUS THEY CONJURE UP. SOUTH FLORIDA CHEFS ALWAYS WORK IN A FIELD OF LOCALIZED *BOLDNESS* THAT IS AMALGAMATED BY THE STABILITY OF OUR COOKERY LEGACY. MUCH OF OUR SOUTH FLORIDA CHEF'S O.J.T. SUBSISTS IN THE "SCHOOL OF FRESHNESS". KEEPING IT LOCAL GUARANTEES FRESHNESS BUT IN SOUTH FLORIDA THIS MEANS THAT MENUS ARE ALWAYS TROPICALLY INFLUENCED.

MUCH OF WHAT WE DO IN SOUTH FLORIDA KITCHENS IS TO REORGANIZE THE PAST. WE UPDATE THE COOKERY OF A MENU TO INCLUDE HEALTHY EXOTIC-TROPICAL ITEMIZED PLATITUDES. CHEFS MAKE THEIR MENUS SIGNIFICANTLY MORE MODERN IN THEIR PRESENTATION AND UPDATE THE ingredients to cultivate a feeling of luxury. Composition of South Beach menus are by nature chic, but we always remember our past to set the goals for our future.

Does it have a clear and distinct Voice?

Your ideals should clamour your cookery style to diners. In South Florida, it is the tropical-exoticness that is unmistakable.

Throughout the United States there are regional cuisines that bellow "soul-food" or "fresh from the farm". Your menu should highlight these tendencies by focusing the printed copy imprint and through communications from your staff to the patrons. This is where a well educated staff helps chefs enlighten the customers to his idealization.

Bringing your staff into the loop will help you educate your patrons so they can understand the reasoning of your menu aspirations. It is with dedicated and protracted discourse that your ideals will be defined to your servers. Every chef has to have a mouthpiece (your staff), enable yours to work in union with your ideals.

Describe the flavors and special cookery techniques with verbose flourishments. Your words have to convince the listener that your amorousness will transpose to them.

Describing cookery techniques will have to be in technical terms yet; you should fabricate the progression heatedly. In surveying your words for positive and fun cookery evolutionary remarks, try to add intricate descriptions that sound enjoyable.

Your Voice.
Your Ideals.

Turmoil abounds around you. Heat, suffocating humidity and a heart pumping work-pace is more like a summertime cardo workout in the gym than it is a day of work at your chosen profession.

Chosen is the optimal word. Most young chefs dream of being that new star on the TV horizon-where all of America knows your name but, it means putting your mind and body through a rigorous workout every day.

Becoming that celebrated chef takes people listening, approving and then buying into your ideals. In advance of molding and shaping your own culinary voice, the uneasiness that you feel because you do not have your own voice is painful. It will only be built after years of day to day experiences.

When you begin to shape your own culinary voice, listen for advice from others. Identity creation will follow you through the rest of your cooking years.

Ask a mentor what they have taught others and then think of ways in which you might follow their conduct. Take *relevant* advice from everyone, shape it using your own manners structuring a renewed voice. Listen to your customers, because "if you only cook what you like to eat, you might be the only one left in your place eating", say chefs I have interviewed for this book. This will help shape your own localized cookery style. The manner in which you get to your objective might change, yet your ideals should remain constant.

Time and time again, I have changed my style according to the position I held. Every new position you take will query your culinary style. Some people want your voice to be bold and new, others want it to conform to their perceived style. It is up to you how to proceed. I always take the bold approach when taking on a new position. I always survey the field for the new and different, experimenting and growing my own personal repertoire.

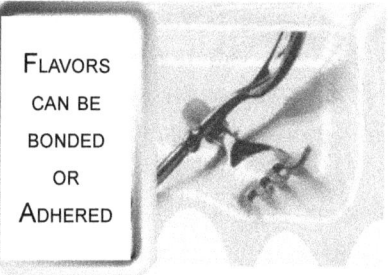

Flavors can be bonded or adhered

When you settle your own culinary ideal and voice, tell it to others. Continuously persuade and remind management and your staff why you think this is the best way of proceeding towards this eatery's new culinary mark.

As you are teaching your staff, ask if they understand. Then ask them to repeat that understanding back to you. Measure it for accuracy, correct their interpretations and then proceed to add more information. As it becomes evident that your style has been the right choice for this eatery, get management to buy into your model and become a part of it. Listen to your staff's input and measure what and why they are telling it. Learn what modifications the customers thirst for and use their point of view to plan.

Although many chefs will tell you their way is the best, it is common sense that should drive your ideal conceptions based upon the customer base you desire. Different diners have dissimilar expectations and requirements.

After the employee buy-in, your staff will more likely become a part of your ideals and then mentor new staff members and the customers to see that *their* enhancements to your ideals succeed more substantially.

Read other chef's cookbooks. See how the authors communicate their culinary ideals and knowledge through the words that were written. The more you can understand the various ways people have tried to communicate their ideals to others, the easier it is for you to do the same.

Restart your thinking as you read. How was it written, what points were made apparent and how did he describe his points to make his ideals obvious to you? Do these words help you understand the author's overall cookery thesis and does he detail his thoughts well enough so anyone can understand?

Inform your staff on comparisons between your ideals and those of published authors giving examples pertaining specifically to items on your menu. Tell them how they should do the same when speaking to the guests at the table. Lay it out simply. Display and prove to the staff how by communicating these ideals their pocketbook will flourish. Use these techniques by launching into an expeditious role-playing scenario. I always do this with one dollar bills in my pocket. Whenever the staff members answer a question the way I want them to, I give them a buck. Repeat this for the entire meeting. Rewards show them that when they work or accomplish tasks your way, everyone wins.

Concerning your Voice....

The most robust way to opine your culinary tag is to unmitigatedly inform mankind of your ideals and cookery imprint.

Adapt your voice about food and dining to include and highlight what practicable concepts mentors have touched upon throughout your career. Informing others about your style, that it is a part of a history of culinary prudence, gives you warranted creditability. There are many examples of this in chef driven culinary books where an author generates a time line tracking famous chefs and their now famous protégés.

Recounting how you gleaned your insights that parallel other successful restaurateurs, will make it easy for them to understand your ideals and that they belong to a bigger picture of culinary history. Keep your discoveries real and simple to understand.

Wear your voice on your sleeve. Make it your predominant working ecosystem. Everything you do ought to simulate your ideals. Getting your staff to follow and mimic your ideals might be a little harder. When Charlie Trotter leaves his restaurant to participate in various culinary events, he knows his restaurant is still running according to his ideals. His staffs conform to his ideals because they live them every day. Chef Trotter started long ago to daily instil and ordain his business values into the staff. Never modifying, never letting an imperfection corrupt his ideals and value system is the compulsion that inspires the staff. Unmask your ideals to staffers regarding your cookery style with gallant memorandums as your vocabulary moves staffers to opt-in to your feelings. In these memos, provide your staff with the proper culinary vocabulary and insights to speak to their customers. You want your staff to sound intelligent about the menu they are representing for you. The more their customers believe in what they are hearing the more sales will increase and the more you will generate that "word of mouth" publicity that we all seek.

LISTEN TO YOUR INNER SELF.

What is important to you should be what is important to others that represent you. Tell people through your writing what your ideals are by first searching deep within yourself.

All of us know when we are being true to our ideals. Whether it is keeping the kitchen clean according to the regulations of a governing body or, "should I aspire to my own higher level?" Listen for that little voice within you when it says, "you can do better". Push towards that voice's goal setting relevance. Do what you know is right. It always works out for the best. You know there are reasons why a cooking process has to be done the way you were taught. You have a strict adherence to the rules because you are dealing with dangerous health concerns. Food is easily mistreated and made dangerous with mishandling. Listen to that voice in your head and remember it is there for the same reason that the health department is.

CONNECTING WITH PEOPLE.

Paint a picture with your words. Describe your culinary ideals in a way that the reader can "feel" your passion for food and cooking. Writers that have constant contact with the public tell of keeping recipes easy and simple. Describe your thoughts well enough so the readers see a picture of what you are describing through the words you are writing.

Use plenty of descriptive words like: "this mango's hue seems to have been beautifully applied by a Monet calibre artist". This is what sets you apart as a communicator. The ability of people to understand your passion through the words that you convey will make you a better idealist.

While formatting your writing, add your own personal discoveries and creative impulses. These are the times when your best discoveries are generated. Remember who your reader is. Generate words that are easy for the reader to understand. Write to the level of the reader, explain in constrained degrees how they can replicate what they are reading. After describing several cookery strategies, you will find that it begets the recipe's development and that is how to describe it. Validate the processes as though the recipe's evolution is occurring immediately in front of you.

- This is when your thoughts really come into play. Make it interesting enough so others want to follow along and learn.

- Build a story using your cookery knowledge to help others to understand why you are telling them to do it your way.

- Give an opening statement in the beginning of the recipe that draws attention. List a rationale why the person should continue to read this recipe by rationalizing the use of a special ingredient or cookery process.

- You could portray a special or unusually stunning tastes stemming from the region where it was grown. Perhaps you fabricated this recipe by mistake and it became a more superior recipe than what you were attempting.

Your Culinary Collections - Your Recipes.

- **You are sharing your passion.**
Your recipes should show your passion for the food used within them. Food writers try to keep the recipes simple for the home cook to make knowing they

DON'T HAVE THE ADVANTAGES THAT WE DO IN RESTAURANT KITCHENS.

> *THE MOST IMPORTANT OUTCOME IS THAT THE RECIPE HAS TO TASTE GREAT.*

WRITING A RECIPE IS A PERSONAL THING. YOUR *CULINARY VOICE* IS AS PERSONAL AS ANY *IDEAL* YOU CARRY WITH YOU ACROSS YOUR CAREER. MAKE YOUR VOICE RING OUT IN THE FRESHNESS AND QUALITY OF THE FOODSTUFFS THAT YOU USE. THE SLOW FOOD MOVEMENT IN SOUTH FLORIDA HAS BEEN ADVOCATING THIS FOR MANY YEARS. RECENTLY IT HAS CAUGHT ON IN A BIG WAY BUT, THE IDEA OF USING THE FRESHEST LOCALLY HARVESTED FOODS AVAILABLE IS CENTURIES OLD. LOCAL FARMER'S MARKETS ARE BUSTLING ALL OVER SOUTH FLORIDA AS CHEFS ARE USING LOCAL FARMERS MORE AND MORE EVERY DAY.

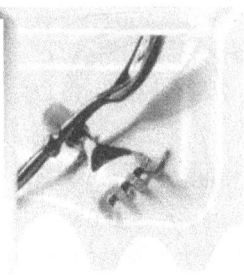

FLAVOR BORROWING OR BLASTING YOUR TASTEBUDS

THE ABILITY TO SHARE YOUR PASSION AS AN ARTIST RINGS TRUE WHEN GOING OVER AND ABOVE WHAT OTHERS WILL DO TO PROVIDE A QUALITY MEAL. THE MORE YOUR PASSION DRIVES YOU, THE MORE NATURAL IT BECOMES TO BE YOUR BEST.

> *DRIVEN BY OUR PASSIONS WE ARE THE UNMISTAKABLE IN THE CULINARY COMMUNITY.*

CULINARY PASSION:

IT IS NOT JUST A JOB, IT IS A MISSION. IT IS A CALLING OF ARTISTS TO FORGE SOMETHING INCREMENTALLY GREATER.

- YOU ARE SHARING A PART OF YOUR KNOWLEDGE AND SKILL.

Food and its preparation are a part of your life. Make sure that people recognize your passion for artistic culinary skill from the words you use as you write a recipe road map.

Imparting one's knowledge is what every chef wants to do when writing a recipe. All chefs have perspectives personalized to their own cookery skills. Giving of one's own experiences is what we do every day with our staffs. Every tutored culinary disciple is different. Each comes with differing levels of compulsory experiences. You have to be able to anticipate the level of experience of those you are teaching and place the correct instruction levels in front of them.

It is important to remember that a reader's comprehension is as important as your recipes.

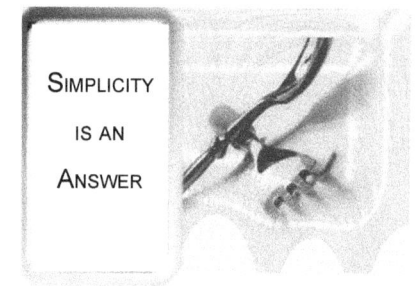

Simplicity is an Answer

- **You are sharing your love of flavors.**

Your communiqué should transmit your passion for the *flavors* you are applying in your recipes. Searching for new flavors is the leading reason why people search out new cookbooks. Make their decision an easy one by speaking from your heart, so people can be affected by your enthusiasm. Sharing your knowledge is a perfect way to quickly draw in the reader's attention...

CHAPTER FOUR:

~FLAVORS~

DRAW OUT AND EVOLVE THE FLAVOR OF A SINGLE OR A TROVE OF INNUMERABLE INGREDIENTS

WHAT WOULD YOU LIKE TO EXPRESS....

CREATIVE FREEDOM OR CONFORMITY TO STANDARDS IS WHAT DEFINES US AS CHEFS. BACK IN THE 1970'S, CONFORMITY TO *FRENCH CLASSICAL* CULINARY TRADITIONS WAS THE ONLY WAY CHEFS WERE EXPECTED TO COOK. NOW, IT IS UNIFORMLY ACCEPTED THAT BEING DIFFERENT IS THE NEW NORMAL. AMERICA'S CHEFS ARE EXPRESSING THEIR INDIVIDUALITIES MORE THAN ANY TEENAGER I KNOW.

CREATIVE FREEDOM IS WHAT EVERY HOMEMAKER LOOKS FOR WHEN SHE BUYS A NEW COOKBOOK. A NEW THEME OR IDEA ABOUT COOKING A FAMILY STANDARD DIFFERENTLY IS WHY WE ALL BUY COOKBOOKS. COOKBOOKS FOR ME ARE JUST A STARTING POINT IN MY EXPLORATIONS TOWARDS TONIGHT'S DINNER. EXPRESS YOURSELF CONTRARILY AND YOUR OWN TASTES WILL DRIVE TO DEFINE YOU AS A CHEF.

Flavors that deliver bold excitement are what culinary dreams are made of. This is why I make my home in South Florida. It is the unprecedented culinary freedoms that are wantonly applied to a chef's life stream which makes it so exciting. It is also the reason why so many trend-setting casts of chefs have their own outpost in South Florida. Due to the influx of chefs and of transplanted northern residents, it seems as though Miami ought to be New York City's sixth borough. These chefs have all found that the creative freedom of South Florida fuels their chief resident restaurant menus with new and exciting combinations of exotic foods and flavors.

Coupling of Flavors

Getting flavors to meld around each other is how I experiment with new recipes. Each chef has his own ideals of how flavors should bond.

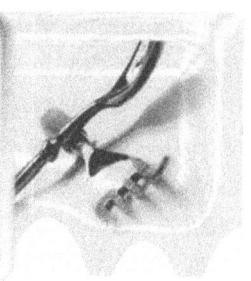

Some food combinations are just right

A bonding example I employ is something called a "Coulis-grette". A "Coulis-grette" is a technique that uses a puree (usually fruit) and adding vinegar to heighten the *sassiness* of the puree and then the oil to smooth out its palatability. Taking a portion of mango puree and mixing it with vinaigrette to create the perfect match for a grilled Yellowtail snapper is one way I get flavors to bond. The sassy acidic taste of the vinaigrette brings out the citrusy notes in the mango, while the clean yet buttery tasting imported extra virgin olive oil enriches the sauce for the same purpose when you construct a beurre blanc. Without the acidic additions, the mango flavor is not as vocal in the recipe.

Another bonding would be when a chef uses the proteins of the egg yolk to hold together ingredients like an emulsion. The yolk bonds to unmixable items and sometimes becomes the preeminent flavor profile for the recipe. Mayonnaise is this perfect example. What would you have without the bonding custardy egg yolk flavor? A vinaigrette! I use this same technique in a few of the coulis-grettes that are my daily repertoire. Recently, because of the health concerns of my guests, I have changed these techniques to bring in some molecular gastronomy by using pre-cooked vegetable starches and gum base thickeners to bond flavors instead of the yolk of an egg.

Bonding of flavors is also recommended and adhered to by classical cooks. What would an oven roasted leg of lamb be like without the addition of rosemary? Or another classic, what would apple tartin be without a caramel sauce? The flavors bond when cooking

and seem as though they couldn't be thought of separately. I could not prepare my favorite demi-glace without the addition of the tamarind. The acidic prune flavor of tamarind (the main ingredient in Worcestershire sauce) enhances a demi glace like nothing else.

Bonding makes the difference in every chef's culinary ideal. It is the way they think things should be paired together, i.e...basil has to go in tomato sauce and Key lime pies should be paired with a meringue topping. Or the opposite of bonding ideals: dairy cheese doesn't go on top fillets of fish.

Symmetry of Flavors

It is not as much as getting one flavor to meld to another but getting them to equalize between each other. Entire books can be written about this....

The perfect example of balance is when my Sous chefs propose a new dish. I quickly taste the combinations of flavors in my mind. Sometimes they choose the wrong combinations and the flavors that contrast too much.

I want the flavors they add to enhance the foods they are cooking not overwhelm or hide the food's original tastes. If they start with a rich fillet of Seabass, then they need to pair it with a slightly acidic sauce. This is the art of Yin and Yang. That is the art of balancing flavors.

It was said to me many times when I was being schooled, "The difference between a chef and a cook is being able to season correctly. Seasonings are in your pantry to heighten the original taste of the food you are about to cook, not be the main flavor in the dish". Chefs tell me this more than any other tutors I have had in my decades of culinary training. It is more about a *respect for* food. Not to over flavor the thing you are cooking but, just nudge it a little so the flavors are dazzling instead of dull.

Taste Great and Does it Give Pleasure?

Seasoning is not flavoring. Flavoring foods is to pair something that will complement the original taste and be noticed as a well deserved addition to the original food's taste. A great example of this is when I learned how to make a *pomme a dora* sauce. We took fresh, very ripe tomatoes, chopped them and sautéed them quickly with a little garlic and fresh virgin olive oil. The oil enhanced the acidic-sweet tomatoes and lent its own astringent-buttery flavor to the entire dish. The recipe's Yin and Yang was based upon the play of the acidic tomatoes counter-balanced by the purity of the buttery olive oil. There was no blending or overcooking the sauce. It was always made to order, tossed together right as the pasta was lifted out of the boiling, salted water.

The oil was generously poured on after the noodles went into the saute pan, so they could absorb the tomato flavor first. The addition and balance of the oil's richness made the dish complete.

"Like Deserves Like" while Balancing Flavors....

When you pair similar tasting elements in a dish, they bond as the food is cooked. I think the same can be exemplified with tuna. When it is wood-fire grilled, the flesh can truly be enhanced with an addition of naturally-brewed soy sauce. Although the meatiness of the tuna is dull, it is improved by the grilling over wood. The soy, used sparingly with the fish, enhances the astringent taste of the grill's char-effect. The soy sauce, if it is a good one, is naturally brewed and cast for fermentation in charred oak barrels for up to six months. The char from the oak barrel's flavor mixes in the fermentation stage and enhances the soy sauce which helps pair the char enhancement from the wood-fire grill. "Like deserves like".

Oven roasted meats deserve the same pairing techniques of pairing similar flavors.

When you roast a joint of beef, you place it over a natural rack of vegetables (a Mirepoix), so while the meat cooks, the juices that escape from the roast drips down into the veggies and caramelize from the heat of the oven. At the same time these vegetables also absorb flavors from the roasting beef above. Then this mirepoix is used to add flavor to the demi glace (sauce) that is paired with the beef when it is served. The rich, caramelized flavors from the natural sweetness of the roasted veggies, enhances the demi glace after it is lifted (deglazed with an addition of wine) from the bottom of the roasting pan. All the caramelized juices left over from the roasting of the beef are scraped up while deglazing to add flavor to the demi-glace which in turn enhances the flavor of the

ROASTED (OVEN-CARAMELIZED) MEAT.
~ "LIKE DESERVES LIKE".

LOANED VERSUS ORIGINAL FLAVOR

TRUE FLAVORS ARE WHAT FOODS TASTE LIKE RAW. AFTER YOU APPLY ANY COOKERY TECHNIQUE TO FOOD, IT CHANGES ITS TASTES, TEXTURES AND THE TRIGIDIMAL EFFECTS ON YOUR BRAIN.

BORROWED FLAVORS HAPPEN AS WE COOK. COOKING IS THE WAY WE TREAT FOODS TO MAKE THEM MORE EASILY CONSUMED. COOKING BY ACID OR HEAT CHANGES THE NATURE OF AND THE FLAVOR OF ANY FOOD. WHAT WOULD BBQ BE LIKE WITHOUT THE TASTE OF A SMOKEY GRILL? WHAT WOULD CEVICHE BE WITHOUT THE ACID COOKING ELEMENT OF LIME JUICE? - SUSHI, RIGHT!

FLAVORS ARE IMPORTANT TO FOOD. IF WE ONLY ATE FOOD IN ITS NATURAL STATE, CUISINE WOULD NOT HAVE BECOME A REALITY. AS FOODS COOK, MOST OF THE NATURALLY OCCURRING MOISTURE WITHIN THE PROTEIN IS LOST AND FINDS ITS WAY INTO THE COOKING PAN. IN MOST

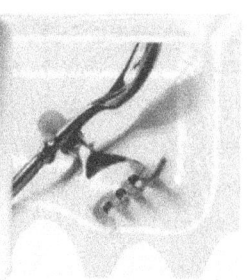

BLAST YOUR TASTEBUDS RIGHT BACK TO THE PAST

CIRCUMSTANCES, THESE JUICES WILL CARAMELIZE BECAUSE YOU ARE USING HEAT TO BREAK DOWN THE TISSUES OF THE FLESH TO MAKE THEM EASIER TO CHEW AND DIGEST. THIS OCCURRENCE LENDS ITSELF TO THE BUILDING OF A FLAVORFUL SAUCE BY DEGLAZING THE ROASTING PAN, TO RELEASE THESE FLAVORS INTO A SAUCE THAT YOU CREATE AFTER THE ROASTING PROCESS. BORROWED FLAVORS ARE THOSE THAT ARE LENT, VIA THE COOKING PROCESS, TO IMPROVE THE FINAL TASTE OF THE DISH.

BORROWED FLAVORS CAN ALSO BE A PART OF THE PRECOOKING MARINADE OR SPICE RUB THAT EVENTUALLY BURNS OFF YET THEIR FLAVORS REMAIN NOTICEABLE. THESE BORROWED FLAVORS ARE THOSE THAT ARE COMPOSED TO ENHANCE THE COOKING AND MIGHT HELP THE DISH GO TOWARDS A FINAL DESTINATION, PERHAPS LIKE ROSEMARY.

Fresh rosemary is extremely strong and has to be dealt with a deft hand. Rosemary comes to its full potential when heated in a super hot skillet and toasted before chopping. The naturally occurring oil in the leaves heats up and escapes into the pan and burns, leaving a great smelling kitchen and a better sauce or marinade because the escaping oil is unfettered as soon as the rosemary is introduced to the procedure. An example of the *borrowed* affect to food is one where you cook a lamb leg. The toasted rosemary enhances the cooked final product, yet is subtle enough so the true, stronger taste of the lamb reveals itself.

Borrowed flavors can also be illustrated in the caramelizing of an onion before you make onion soup. Caramelizing the onion to brown the soup gives it an enriched natural sweetness. The borrowed flavor of the caramelizing effect enhances the eye appeal and the character of the final product.

Wilful Intensity – Brazen Dishes that "Bite" the Senses....

South Florida chefs used to blast your taste buds with a conspiracy of taste, meant to blow up your brain's taste receptors.

In 1995, when New World Cuisine (NWC) was going strong, it was a blast-your-taste buds effect that everyone sought. Now the cookery maxim is to use great tasting flavor enhancements that do not override the original flavors of the foods you are cooking. Blasting your taste buds has taken the same course as French Classical Cuisine. The thousands of *classic* sauces evolved to façade the taste of a low quality food. Not to say South Florida chefs dealt with less quality products, the original true flavors were just hidden, like many dishes in French Classical cuisine. Now, the need to jolt your taste buds into unconsciousness, outdistance our singular fresh from the sea flavors.

REAL DELICIOUSNESS - SWEETNESS VS. SUBTLETY.

I HAVE ALWAYS FOUND THAT FOODS WITH NATURAL SWEETNESS ARE MORE ACCEPTED BY MY GUESTS. THIS DOESN'T DICTATE THAT SWEETNESS GOES WITH EVERYTHING. I AM JUST SAYING AMERICANS ARE USED TO FOODS THAT ARE A LITTLE MORE SWEET THAN SAVORY. CHECK EVERY PACKAGED FOOD CONTAINER IN YOUR REFRIGERATOR OR PANTRY. LOOK FOR NATURAL SWEETENERS LIKE CORN SYRUP OR GLYCOLS — WHICH ARE SWEET ALCOHOL CHEMICAL COMPONENTS.

I HAVE FOUND THAT SWEETNESS IN RECIPES HAS TO BE DELIVERED WITH A FEATHER-LIGHT HAND. NATURAL SWEETNESS IS EXPECTED AND WHEN IT ISN'T WHERE IT IS EXPECTED, DISAPPOINTMENT FOLLOWS. FOODS THAT ARE DELICIOUS AREN'T NECESSARILY SWEET, YET WHO WOULD SAY THAT A CREAMY-SWEET CRÈME BRULEE OR THAT VELVETY-LIGHT CHOCOLATE MOUSSE ISN'T DELICIOUS.

SWEETNESS IN OTHER PLACES IS A NICE CHANGE OF PACE. A PERFECTLY RIPE TOMATO OR A JUST-PICKED GREEN BEAN HAS A LIGHT SWEETNESS TO THEM. MANY FRUITS, AND A FEW VEGETABLES, ARE THOUGHT OF THIS WAY. I WILL TAKE A TOO SAVORY DISH AND BALANCE THE TOTAL PLATE TASTE FOR MY GUESTS BY ADDING A LITTLE NATURALLY SUBTLE SWEETNESS. I FIND THAT EVERYONE LOVES THE COUNTER-BALANCE OF A MANGO SALSA SET BESIDE A SAVORY AND ZESTFUL PRESENTATION OF CARIBBEAN-SPICED GROUPER. IT IS THE YIN-YANG BALANCE I STRIVE FOR IN EACH PLATE. IT IS MORE THAN COMMON NOWADAYS TO HAVE ONE RECIPE ON THE PLATE THAT IS SAVORY AND ANOTHER THAT IS BLAND OR MARKED WITH JUST A HINT OF SWEETNESS. IT IS THE BALANCE AND COUNTER BALANCE THAT A CHEF SHOULD AIM FOR TO COMPLETE A SINGULAR GOAL OF A PLEASURABLE DINING EXPERIENCE.

FREE-FORMING YOUR IDEALS

Finding the Simplicity in the Intricate. When a chef speaks about his philosophy of cuisine, it is this peripheral accentuated culinary ideal of how he balances flavors that allures. A perfect illumination of this is when a chef speaks about grilling the simplest herb roasted Yellowtail Snapper. He portrays the dish as vaguely seasoned with sea salt, cooked and served perfectly fresh on the plate with little alterations, as if it came out of the Atlantic Ocean.

Digging deep into your thoughts it is this a-ha moment when a light bulb pops on, yeah that is the way I think too, that makes your robust probing through cookbooks beneficial. Balance, a treasured commodity of using a deft hand at seasonings and, pairing seasonings to foods is not a hereditary talent. We need the effortless to balance our thoughts about the complex. We as chefs strive for the *Unami* of a recipe and a consistently satisfied customer.

Whether ideals of cuisine is strict adherence to previous culinary styling or not, sometimes it just feels good to step outside the boundaries.

The simple pleasure of natural sweetness from a pineapple endears itself to me. I can say the same about mangos with their complexity of flavors that are subtle yet complex in vastness. A mango can taste of citrus, turpentine, apple, quince, pineapple, guava or a peachy-carrot yet, all are significant to the recipe that they are added to because of these taste-variances. The simplicity is that all mangos have similar great "mango" taste in common yet still the subtleties in the unannounced differences is what draws attention. Assessing the tastes of a mango is similar to a horizontal wine tasting. All Cabernets frequently have similar taste profiles yet all have differing taste nuances from their growing elements. Growing conditions, soil, weather changes and harvesting methods make vivid contrasts to each connoisseur. There are so many differing nuances in a single variety of wine that it takes years to train your palette to recognize the subtlety. These differences are the reason why we all enjoy wine.

As chefs we each have our individual favorite flavoring techniques and it is these slight differences that consumers appreciate. The caliber of and, the level of culinary competence shown to a specific cookery heritage, trend or ideal that you tout, is how many people choose where to dine. It is called a niche or a calling. We as chefs know it as the most effortless way to do things.

My style is habitually cooking the foods that are uncommon yet, easily and locally sourced from across South Florida. I find it easy to implement a "Caribb-ican" cookery style because of the ease of finding tropical foods living in South Florida. And since we live in the vicinity of the Caribbean, this lifestyle begets my zealous approach to cook with a Caribbean reach.

Cooking in the Caribbean can be trying on the taste buds. In South Florida we moderate the heat of the tropics with the permissiveness of a South Beach imprint. We cook with prudence in the era of a Facebook society and it is now with a light touch that South Florida chefs push your taste buds to a Caribbean familiarity. The cookery is lighter and fresher than in years past. We live by the sword and die by the scimitar of subtropical inclination.

Florida, being America's second leading agricultural state, most of our modern-day menus are produce driven, after the fresh seafood entree superstar, just as many of the Caribbean's vast cookery heritages are produce driven.

In the Caribbean, plates are filled with a plethora of starch and vegetable food products because of the economy of garden-raised foodstuffs. Proteins are always higher in price per pound so, you will see the simplicity of more veggies on the Caribbean table. Necessity of life has now morphed into a heritage of cookery.

Simply stated, it is easier to cook something for dinner that is cheaper on the wallet.

Communion of Ingredients

Natural is better. Of course things that occur as a matter of course in nature are going to be better when they are balanced together on a plate. Take seasalt and seafood. When you crust a whole fish, like a Yellowtail snapper in Sea salt and fresh rosemary or thyme, the resulting cooked dish will be simplistic perfection.

Pairing "like" tasting items together makes a good culinary matrimony. Take the Asian "Holy Trinity" - powdered ginger, wasabi and soy sauce. The potent combination of pairing powdered ginger with the vibrant wasabi and the addition of a salty soy sauce facilitates a flavor-fusion that brings all their flavor-factors together to play well together as an united team.

Speaking of savory, some of my best meals have been while creating a commune of flavorful herb bouquets (like rosemary, sage and thyme) and using it as a rub to marinate food before cooking.

Remember that a sauce component is as important as any other seasoning you can add to a plate. The addition of cream to a sauce has its advantages. As you use cream in a sauce, it helps chefs keep the protein amount of the plate to a minimum and still give the diner a fulfilling subtlety. In the dish of Steak Diane, a small portion of beef is coated with a sauce made of demi-glace and cream. As the cream evens out the puissance of a stout demi-glace, it coats the lining of your stomach and the sensors in the stomach lining will tell your head that it is full. So, the use of cream and butter for enriching a dish is actually a money saver for your kitchen because you ultimately use less of the premium priced protein in the recipe.

The classic salsa is Mother Nature's most versatile healthy- flavor enhancer. Fruit salsas being sweet and spicy at the same time can go as a flavorful compliment for so many entrees.

Flavor and good-for-you natural communion is a healthy flavor levitation alternative to enrich the taste of a dish without an unhealthy annexation of butter fats. When dealing with a light, white-meat protein, the use of salsas is thought of as a culinary birthright for South Florida chefs.

Value in the Quintessential... Does this mean complexity in garnishing?

Adding a side dish to the protein is the easy part. Working in the appropriate tasting garnishment, one with a specific counter balance that makes the entire preparation successful, is an assignment that takes extra perseverance.

Chefs have this talisman tied around their necks as surely as a chef's neckerchief. Most restaurants during difficult economic times have found that giving value means plates full of food. In other distinguished dining halls, fanciful plate presentations are largely revered. People eat with their eyes first so, both effects each consumer's differing rationale. The one person sees that he is going to be brim full after eating so much food. Others take pleasure in the awe of the finesse in the artful presentation and they value its uniqueness over the plate's volume. Both will be happy with their discriminate experience as their expectations are met or exceeded.

I have always felt that we as chefs should go the latter route. The artful presentation, minimal in its total content of food on the plate, yet so beautiful that people hesitate to eat without snapping a picture first, is the real dining value.

Dining in any metropolitan area of our country, you will find that this rings true. The chefs that I have interviewed agree in most cases. No matter the volume on the plate, when it looks fantastic on the plate, that is the best dining value for the dollar. "It is all in the garnishment", says my lecturing chef at the Culinary Institute. Small amounts of refined garnitures bring value to any plate presentation. It is the simplicity in economy that most of us look to achieve by the customer's recognition of the complexity in simplistic accomplishments-a beautiful plate!

Culinary Aesthetics - If it tastes delicious, does it give joy?

What does the grandeur of being the chef mean? Did they become "grand chefs" because of the deliciousness of their food or, is it that they produced grand recipes because of the people that they are already? I think it is the latter in most cases.

Let us look at Chef Charlie Trotter's restaurant in Chicago. His culinary ideals manage the restaurant in a more than successful manner, as the media touted his efforts, which made him the grand chef we all know. Charlie brought to the fold that there is never a minute detail nonchalant enough to overlook. Charlie is that person. A detailed orientated personality, that insists on delivering attention to all aspects of the dining experience. When it comes to his success, pleasing the guest and going above their expectations was crucial in the decades of his restaurant's integral success. Everyone from the pot washers to the waiters knows this is the only goal in his restaurant.

Every day, if the guest doesn't think the food is right, then no matter what others think about the grand cuisine, it is not right. It is always meeting and then exceeding expectations that makes a formidable chef.

Taste is relative. With this emphasis, Charlie Trotter might be a great chef and his food has been highly praised across the culinary spectrum but, when the guest says it doesn't tastes right to him, then it is not right. No matter who cooked it, right or wrong.

Delicious is relative. If you cannot judge a person's taste contention by looking at him, then it is almost impossible to make food suited to every person. Some cultures can't stand meats that are rare or medium-rare, so this means that some foods will always be cooked improperly according to our culinary tradition. But in the opinion of the diner, it is not cooked correctly so it isn't delicious. If it pleases some cultures to eat duck breast or tuna loin steak well done, so be it. If it gives them pleasure, it is right.

So who is right, the chef that goes to any length to provide whatever the customer wants or the chef that tries to educate the diner to what he thinks is the proper way to cook and consume food?

Pioneered Synthesis

The pioneering of a *culinary synthesis* is how you bend and reshape idiomatic cookery standards to a not yet reached superlative. It is the continued

SUBSTITUTION AND PROTRACTION OF IDEALS AND INGREDIENTS BY PAIRING THE UNFAMILIAR WITH THE COMMONLY TRUSTED.

WEBLINK TO MY BLOG ABOUT COOKING IN SOUTH FLORIDA.

IN SOUTH FLORIDA THIS IS NOT ONLY COMMON, IT IS A CHEF'S WAY OF LIFE. WE ARE FREE OF THE REIGNS THAT HOLD BACK OTHER CHEFS. MOST CHEFS HAVE TO OPERATE RESTAURANTS WITH REINS THAT CONSTRAIN A CHEF'S FREEDOMS BY DEPLOYING STRICT ADHERENCE TO A FORMAL CULINARY HERITAGE THAT SKETCH OUT HOW TO COOK RECIPES ACCORDING TO WHAT HAS BEEN DONE IN THE PAST. OUR SOUTH FLORIDA CUISINE IS ONE OF INVENTION. WE AS CHEFS ARE BY NATURE CURIOUS. THIS IS SOMETHING THAT ISN'T HELD IN CHECK WHEN YOU COOK IN SOUTH FLORIDA.

BE TRUE TO YOURSELF AND BECOME YOUR OWN MERLIN IN YOUR KINGDOM OF INNOVATION.

WITH YOUR BACKYARD FILLED WITH EXOTIC TROPICAL FRUIT, IT IS NOT HARD TO COMPREHEND WHY SOUTH FLORIDA CHEFS ARE SO EXPERIMENTAL. THE EVER-PRESENT INFLUX OF NEW FOODS TO EXPERIMENT WITH COMES BY WAY OF A KNOCK ON YOUR BACK DOOR FROM THE LOCAL FARMER. THIS WON'T HAPPEN DAILY BUT, IT IS COMMON TO HAVE A HAGGLING LOCAL PRODUCE FARMER CALL TWO TIMES A WEEK WANTING TO SELL YOU THEIR LATEST HARVEST OF ATEMOYA, MANGO OR CANISTEL.

CHEFS SHOULD ALWAYS TEST WHAT A PREVIOUSLY CONCEIVED NOTION OF WHAT CUISINE IS AND ADVOCATE WHAT IT CAN BE.

ONCE YOU ARE KNOWN BY THE LOCALS AS AN INNOVATOR THAT USES LOCALLY GROWN EXOTIC PRODUCTS, THE CALLS BECOME MORE FREQUENT AND VARIED. THIS AVAILABILITY, TO BRING THE NEW AND DIFFERENT TO THE TABLE DAILY, is what being a chef in South Florida is all about.

Our chefs daily use locally raised herbs, micro greens and unusual amounts of fresh-from-the-farm tropical produce and pairs them with Florida's unending list of seafood and then arranges the outcome with a metropolitan-cuisine frame of mind.

Our unusual cookery style might not have a chronicled culinary heritage that has an easily discernible inheritance yet, it is noteworthy. The significance is in the final recipe's taste. Some might call it con-*fusion* cuisine, in South Florida, we call it home style.

An Awestruck Sense

"Bang" and a handful of capsicum is splashed onto the plate, your taste buds are overstimulated and you are yearning for the Crème Brulee to quiescent your cauterized tastebuds.

Weblink to new cookbook on South Florida cooking

That is no longer a way of life for South Florida chefs.

The big-bang theory was good to get South Florida cuisine noticed by food enthusiasts across the foodie world but, I opine with reservation. The big-bang culinary ideal hides the stunning and delicate nuances of our seafood and exotic tropical fruit. It was a good way to start the ball rolling but today we will find chefs redefining a definitive flavor complexion rather than reloading for another palette assault.

Today, delicacy is as important as squealing

the tires to catch the diner's scrutiny. A sheep in wolves' clothing can be the way we describe new South Florida cookery. It is seemingly docile yet subtly fulfilling with lush overtones due to our tropically exotic Caribbean influenced cookery gradations.

The syntheses of all of our different cookery styles can be daunting yet still remains acutely engaging for your taste buds. The Spanish flair and usage of starch on the plate is always a great symmetry for the heat from an equatorial Haitian or Jamaican sauce.

Intimate portions served on oversized plates have been the norm for decades in formal dining arenas and chefs love the effect to the bottom line of their P & L's. Our quantum of French culinary training has moved us through yesteryear's nouveau cuisine standards that vaunt copious tendencies of white space on the dinner plate to plates with an architectural imprint.

The French side also calls to a chef's whim to the fanciful and artistic. Classic French cuisine has always been one that bolstered the need for strict adherence. Variety never played a part in the classical kitchen. Today we break the chains of once-tight restrictive form and free form plate presentations that are as abundant as the variety of classic sauces in Le Gastominque. We consider ourselves artists and as such, the rules of adherence should never apply to the heuristically expressive and experimental South Florida chef. Free-form plating and almost mad scientist approach in the kitchen is now the rage.

The classic foodways originating in pre-colonial France are as long forgotten as last year's New Year's Eve resolutions. We strive for the new and different. Being on the cusp of a new culinary standard is the way of the South Florida chef.

CREATIVITY AND COMMON SENSE - *THE IMPORTANCE OF "NO BRAINERS"*

Being creative is what being a chef is all about. Your creativity needs to be counter-balanced against the necessity to make profits. No-Brainers are the recipes that accomplish both ingenuity and profitability.

We try so hard to be at the forefront of the culinary trend that doing the substantial chores that keep the doors open and pay the bills appears like an afterthought. We need no-brainers on our menus, those tried and true, good profit generators and well liked entrees and appetizers that keep everyone happy. Finding that certain something that everyone likes, let's say like pizza ,is that no-brainer. How do you think Wolfgang Puck was so successful? Gourmet pizzas were the melding of great profitability and the culinary positioning of being at the forefront of a new culinary trend.

Chef Michael Bloise has discovered the same opportunities at his new restaurant. The "*Noodle Bar*" is where Chef Michael's latest restaurant venue has produced a no-brainer for creating profits with gourmet noodle dishes.

The *bowls* and *small plates* give his customers the capacity to try an Asian leaning cuisine at an urban price point. Everyone has a great experience and the chef is operating profitably. The noodle bar gives Chef Michael the opportunity to commune with his guests in the open kitchen and the restaurant's variety of recipes keeps him gastronomically stimulated. A no-brainer all around.

The chef wanted to be able to commune with the patrons and see the guest's satisfaction first hand, instead of the chef stuck behind multiple layers of carpentry and stucco.

The restaurant's design was as significant no-brainer as the menu itself.

Efficiency was the no-brainer here. It is almost a one-man show. This efficient exhibition kitchen based restaurant is one of the main draws. Being efficient has brought the chef another no-brainer. He is able to commune with his clientele as they eat in the dining room adjoining the kitchen.

Lose the Boundaries and Molds in South Florida

Boundaries are only made to be broken. As covered earlier, without culinary tradition, chefs would have to reinvent every recipe every time they got behind a sauté pan. This is where we use the term *mold*. The mold is always meant to be broken. What better way to describe what happens behind the stainless bulkhead every day in South Florida kitchens?

Boundaries and this *Mold* are there to help start a chef towards his own unique culinary thesis.

Molds are the foundations which we build upon to create a sublime cookery heritage. When New World Cuisine was in its infancy, South Florida chefs found local farmers willing to surrender their overabundance of tropical crops so chefs could create innovative recipes. The local farmers were proud to fuel the culinary machine known better as *New World Cuisine*, with their epitome foods. So many of my friends in the Rare Fruit Council were happy to give me all their excess fruit so I could experiment and create unique recipes. The culinary fuel was free to many of us who knew the right people, so the engine roared in the 1990's.

The freedom to create is why a chef does what he does. Losing the boundaries of the cost in products gave us the ability to experiment to a greater extent without consequence to the P&L. It was a total no-brainer.

Breaking the mold is what we did every day. Taking the mere swamp cabbage and marinating it in a citrus juice after slicing it thinly, placing on a plate that saw added hints of the Caribbean palate studded with locally harvested mango, starfruit and papaya, it was new and totally out of the box thinking for a summertime salad.

Breaking the mold is what we tried to do every day. It is not just a daily duty, it is a necessity, which the media bestows great press and generates more visit frequency by your customer base. I find that during the era of New World Cuisine (circa: 1992-2002) we held the torch that enumerated: being nascent is the new valor. It takes pride and a sense of valiantry to become a culinary mad scientist experimenting all day every day, to stretch the known universe of culinary boundaries.

An Element of Tryst

A tryst: a clandestine meeting of lovers. The rudiments of a tryst: the chef making love through his cooking.

Today's chef plays a role in South Florida that was unseen just two decades ago. He has become a community leader, an artist and a rebel all in the same breath.

The rebel chef portrays his non-conformist nature through his love of being different in the choices he presents on his menu. Maybe this love affair is his illustrating respect of being different and thus creates an amorous patronage from his clientele. Maybe it is the chef's ability to perform culinary wizardry that engender admiration from his patrons. Or being a leader of the few in his kitchen brigade makes him the perfect choice for leadership roles in the community. Whatever the motive, there is a love affair between chefs and South Floridians

THAT IS HARD TO PORTRAY, EXCEPT TO ASCRIBE IT AS A TRYST.

ACCURATE VERSES RIOTOUS PORTRAYAL AND RULES O' OLD!

NEW AMERICAN REGIONAL COOKERY TAKES WHAT CLASSICAL FRENCH COOKERY TAUGHT US ABOUT RIGID ADHERENCE OF FOOD PREPARATION AND FLIRTS ALONG ITS FRINGES WITH RIOTOUS APATHY. LOOSE REPRESENTATIONS OF CLASSICAL FRENCH TECHNIQUES ARE USED EVERY DAY IN AMERICA'S GREATEST KITCHENS BUT IT IS AT THE FRINGES WHERE OUR CUISINE IS PROMOTED THAT THE ***RULES OF OLD*** ARE BLOCKED OUT.

CREATIVITY DEMANDS LOOSE ADHERENCE TO THE RULES OF OLD. ONCE YOU BREAK AWAY FROM THE EXPECTED, CREATIVITY MUST BE AN EFFECTUAL ROAD MAP FOR YOUR FUTURE. AS IN CREATIVITY, JUST BEING DIFFERENT IS NOT ENOUGH. THERE HAS TO BE A REASON FOR METAMORPHOSIS AND NOT JUST TO FIND NEW CUSTOMERS. CURDLING YOUR CULINARY THEORIES JUST TO CREATE PROFITS ISN'T A BLESSING FOR YOURSELF OR YOUR PROFESSIONAL INTEGRITY. INNOVATION HAS TO MAKE SENSE FOR BOTH SELF RESPECT AND RESPECT OF YOUR PROFESSION.

Chapter Five:

Chefs and Foodies...

That have made Ideals a reality.

A Day in the life of a South Florida Chef.

The coastline of South Florida routinely brings thousands of visitors to our shores each year. It is the relaxing sounds of the pounding surf that always makes it a pleasure to work on the beach. These allures have consistently increased the number of chefs gravitating to this area.

As you cruise to work in your classic red convertible, you notice that the sun has struck you in a slightly different way today. Then you realize today is Monday, the beach has had some time to recoup from the 24 hour, nonstop, weekend party. As you proceed over the last bridge to the beach, you can see five 40 foot racing cigarettes on their way north. As the mist spews out from behind these boats, you can feel a trace of the lingering mist on your face. It is the trappings of millionaire mansions shining like pristine towers of crystal that brings you back from your dreaming and back into reality.

You pull into the final drive up to your "Kingdom du Jour" as two stealth bodies pass in front of you, bumping and weaving through a thickening mass of people. You have inadvertently been treated to shapely aspects of humanity as you find yourself in the throes of a visual perpetual party on the planet. South Beach is where everyone is a model and where all models are waiters. Models, model-wannabes, model-chasers and model-makers will soon pass through your doors to experience something that others span the globe to partake.

As you peruse last night's business with the manager, there has been another VIP guest added to tonight's reservation list. There has been a great influx of Sports, Music industry, Television and Movie personalities to this area. All come to meet and greet in the renovated Art Deco buildings that line this coconut palm tree beach front. It is because of this influx of celebrity that your restaurant has become a popular stop on the "Noshing Tour de Beach".

As the Indian summer sky turns from pale yellow-orange to purple and then to black the throng of people in your restaurant thickens. The blackness of the night is a call to arms for the culinary professionals of South Beach. SoBe is Florida's "Nightlife Capital". Wisps of German, French and Spanish are heard over the multitude in the dining room. All are awaiting the culinary magic and tonight, your name is Merlin.

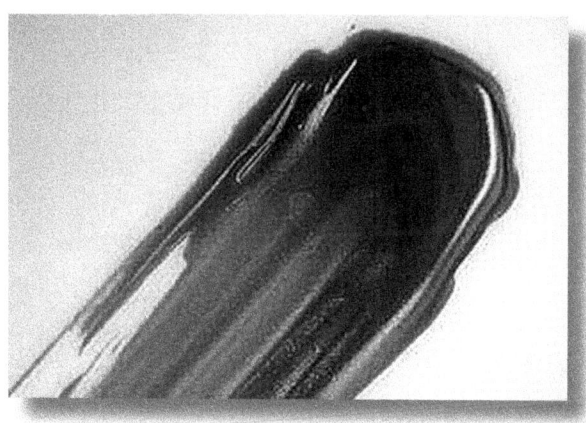

THE PLAYERS

THAT HAVE

"CRAFTED" A CUISINE.

THE PLAYERS:

AGAIN,

...TO ALL THAT I HAVE WORKED WITH IN THE PAST AND TO EVERYONE THAT HAS SHAPED MY VOICE IN THE CULINARY FIELD, **THANKS.**

I WOULD LIKE TO THANK EVERYONE MENTIONED IN THIS BOOK AND THE HUNDREDS OF OTHER FOOD PROFESSIONALS THAT I HAVE WORKED WITH OVER THE LAST TWO DECADES. SOME MENTIONED HERE IN THIS SECTION PLAYED A SIGNIFICANT ROLE IN MY UPBRINGING AS A CHEF. TO ALL THE OTHERS THAT HAVE HELPED IN THIS LIFE-LONG ENDEAVOUR I SAY- **THANKS.** YOUR THOUGHTS ABOUT THE CULINARY PROFESSION AND THE WISDOM THAT I HAVE GLEANED FROM OUR CONVERSATIONS HAVE BEEN INESTIMABLE.

ALPHA CONTEMPORARIES:

CARIBBEAN ISLAND RESTAURANTS:

These island restaurants and chefs' cooking styles were the origin of future generations of South Florida chefs. It is the blueprint cuisine to guide an entire regional profession towards what was to come in the forthcoming decades.

Far off in the distance three island nations that have helped craft a cuisine: Jamaica, Cuba and the Dominican Republic cookery cultures have inspired many of our panoptic Caribbean menus. It was a starting point for many South Florida chefs seeking tips on how to use our locally harvested tropical foods.

Santo Domingo, one of the oldest cities of the New World, located on the island of the Dominican Republic, has one of the Caribbean's largest populations. This city's food and cookery poised much of South Florida's culinary inheritance.

Many non-Miamians think that South Florida is only Cuban-based cuisine. The Dominican Republic is the mother of the other Spanish Caribbean nations as it was wildly fought over throughout the centuries. It was the earliest base for Spain's exploration of the New World as well as being a base for many infamous pirates.

In the modern world, Miami is a sister city for Santo Domingo confirmed largely through our tropically-inspired fare. South Florida has all the common elemental natural attributes of Santo Domingo and our duplication of a profuse selection of seafood is just as commonplace.

The cuisine that reigns in this New World colony stems from Spanish as well as an African ancestry. This Island cuisine was also the basis for Miami's dominate Cuban and Puerto Rican cuisines. South Florida's culinary vibe will always build upon this culinary complexion.

CONCEPTION:

The New World's predominate cuisine is based upon Caribbean, Spanish and the rustic, economy-based cookery of the early 17th century African peoples. The cuisine of the Caribbean Islands revolves around its most abundant foods - produce. Recipes most likely contain a variety of countrified veggies, tubers and starchy foods, fresh from the surrounding ocean's seafood, pork and poultry. Meals are handily rustic in nature because of the use of simple cooking techniques and essential cookery elements. It is a cuisine of economy, where everything from an animal is used and Grandma's recipes reflect this in the family's nightly dinners.

In the Caribbean Islands, grocery stores do not sell pre-cut onions or already roasted chicken like in America. Canned stewed tomatoes were unheard of until just a decade ago. Everything from the rural Caribbean kitchen was fresh from the home's own garden. If Grandma did not pick it that morning, it was not in that evening's meal. The local farmer's market, where Island peoples (belongers) commune, is a place where the callow can go to feel part of authentic Island heritage. These rustic bazaars boast the best products right from a local farmer that unknown to you, might be your next-door neighbor.

FINESSE:

The use of seafood through this culturally predicated culinary art results in your awareness of how simplistically good an exotic tropical cuisine can be. In the Caribbean, fresh seafood means minutes fresh from the ocean waters to the water atop a stove. There have been times in my journeys through the Caribbean that fresh from the ocean meant a small, very aged boat will pull up outside my beachfront restaurant with today's catch of lobsters and wheel barrel them right into your kitchen to be cooked unhesitatingly quickly without reservation.

Production:

This "Old World" cookery culture has been all but extinguished over the centuries. The place where the Old World met the New (South Florida) is the place where a New American cultural dawning has bestowed upon us a lighter, healthier cuisine called New World Cuisine.

As portrayed earlier, our South Florida cookery methodologies will always be based upon others that have come before them. Like any methodology, it was built upon many layers of previous culinary trends and ideologies. Since the 1990's, when New World Cuisine was in vogue, we have annexed many new cookery aspects into a global thought evolution. The foods of South Florida's tropically inspired New World Cuisine were just a basis to develop a new American Regional Cuisine that has reached beyond its original culinary framework.

Yes, our menus always have a tropical feel but, the menu ingredients are now sourced outside the borders of the pan-Caribbean basin. A "Palm-Tree" cuisine, that is one where chefs have brought in food from allocated resources that span globally along latitudinal equivalent nations, has replaced the restrictiveness that New World Cuisine was based upon. This has meant chefs can develop more interesting menu combinations with exotic foods from almost anywhere around the tropical equator.

We see it every day in South Florida; the Japanese-inspired cuisine of Peru has snatched a foothold in Miami. Foods sourced from Asia are manipulated in the cookery traditions of our newest influx of Peruvian and Latin American chefs. The same can be said about restaurants that source products from the equatorial regions of Israel and some neighboring North African nations.

THE NOUVEAU GENERATION:

This generation of Chefs brought the then ever-popular Nouveau culinary traditions to our South Florida shores. It was the era of tiny portions, that were dainty and diminutive, situated deliberately on oversized plates. This generation of chefs gave credence to use of naturally reduced stock which turned into sauces. They were at the apex of delivering locally raised and harvested seafood, game and produce to the South Floridian's plate.

Driven by the need to balance food's taste and appearance on the plate, these chefs delivered to America the love of tropically exotic flavors in neat diminutive packages. The package was a pure and manicured plate of food that was seeing the effects of the newest trend of that decade- Spa Cuisine. Chefs began making foods healthier and lighter with the exclusion of any butterfat and replacing butter's enriching dynamic with fruit salsa and chutneys. Of course, this was perfect for experimental chefs that had South Florida's exotic tropical fruit bounty to employ. It soon became commonplace to see the newfound mango and starfuit of every plate replacing the sliced kiwi and decorative snow pea that predominated a few years prior.

ALLEN SUSSER:
COOKERY BIO:

CHEF ALLEN'S RESTAURANT HAS PROCURED ACCOLADES FROM LOCAL AND NATIONAL FOOD WRITERS: FOOD AND WINE MAGAZINE NAMED ALLEN SUSSER AS ONE OF THE TOP 10 NEW CHEFS IN AMERICA IN 1991. THE NEW YORK TIMES NAMED ALLEN SUSSER "THE PONCE DE LEON OF NEW FLORIDIAN COOKING" AND NOTES THAT SUSSER'S BACKGROUND SPARKED A TIGHTLY FOCUSED NEW AMERICAN REGIONAL CUISINE.

HE HAS REINVENTED HIMSELF AND UPDATED HIS RESTAURANT NUMEROUS TIMES SINCE OPENING CHEF ALLEN'S.

CHEF ALLENS WEBSITE

WEBLINK TO CHEF ALLEN'S COOKBOOK

CHEF ALLEN'S DRAMATIC TRANSLATION OF THE SOUTH FLORIDA'S BOUNTY OF TROPICAL FOODSTUFFS BECAME KNOWN AS *NEW WORLD CUISINE*. IN 1995, HIS INSPIRED AND INNOVATIVE COOKERY SIGNATURE BECAME AN IMPORTANT CONTRIBUTION TO AMERICAN CULINARY ARTISANSHIP. HIS AUDACIOUS FRENCH-INSPIRED CARIBBEAN FOOD MADE WAVES AND BROUGHT HIM THE RANKING AS ONE OF AMERICA'S SUPERSTAR CHEFS. HIS SELF-ENTITLED "NEW WORLD CUISINE" (N.W.C.) COOKBOOK MADE ITS WAY THROUGH SOUTH FLORIDA AND THEN THE REST OF OUR NATION CHEF ALLEN BECAME N.W.C.'S CHAMPION.

THE FOLLOWING DECADES CARRIED CHEF ALLEN'S COOKERY CONSTITUTION TO GYRATE BROADLY TOWARDS A HEALTHY, GLOBALLY BASED "PALM TREE" CUISINE.

THOUGHT PROCESSES:

A NEW ERA OF THINKING...
CHEF ALLEN'S DINERS EXPECT TO DISCOVER SOMETHING MEMORABLE WHEN THEY VISIT THIS ESTABLISHMENT. *NEW ERA* THINKING IS A WORKING FORMULA ROOTED IN THE CLASSIC FRENCH TECHNIQUE, WHICH IS CHEF ALLEN'S ORIGINAL DISCIPLINE. YET, THE CREATIVE PROCESS WITH *NEW ERA* EXTENDS THAT REACH AND BRINGS ORIGINALITY TO ANOTHER LEVEL. THIS *NEW ERA* FOOD PAIRINGS ARE FROM A DIVERSE GLOBAL REGION, MATCHED WITH THE DISCIPLINE OF MAINTAINING THE INTEGRITY AND THEIR MULTICULTURAL HERITAGE CHARACTERISTICS AND COOKERY METHODOLOGIES. THE CHALLENGE OF THE 21ST CENTURY IS HOW TO APPLY THE WORLD'S INGREDIENTS IN A COMPLETELY INNOVATIVE WAY. THE DESIRED RESULT WITH PALM TREE CUISINE — THE AMALGAMATION OF TASTES AND THE USE OF PRODUCTS FROM ANYWHERE IN THE WORLD WHERE A PALM TREE WOULD GROW – FOR A GLOBAL MENU PREMISE IS AN EGALITARIAN EXPRESSION OF OUR GLOBAL VILLAGES' FOODS AND SPICES. MODERN FOOD WILL NOT BE A REFLECTION OF A SINGLE CULTURE. THIS COOKERY PHILOSOPHY ENCOURAGES THE FUSING OF INGREDIENTS FROM MANY CUISINES AND CULTURES.

CULINARY FINESSE:

ALLEN IMMEDIATELY IDENTIFIED SOUTH FLORIDA'S EMPHATIC NATURAL RESOURCES AS A FOUNTAINHEAD FOR A UNIQUE CULINARY FOUNDATION. ADAPTING HIS CULINARY TRAINING AND COOKERY TECHNIQUES IN A CREATIVE AND INQUISITIVE MANNER, HE FOUND HIS *FOUNTAIN OF YOUTH*.

PRODUCTION:

SINCE ITS BIRTH, NEW WORLD CUISINE WAS AND IS TRANSFORMATIVE. ITS FOOD PRODUCTION TECHNIQUES ARE AS WELL. A COMBINATION OF SOLID BASED FOOD PREPARATION MODUS OPERANDI HAS LED TO INTERPOLATED STOVETOP EXPERIMENTATION. IT IS WHERE once commonplace beurre blancs of the 1970's, are now characteristically replaced with lighter, healthy tropical fruit vinaigrette infusions.

Furthermore:

We are now a more health conscious culinary society with all the trappings of a regal convention of nobility. Chefs are thought of today as august, their techniques are referred to with admiration by guests. This is the lifestyle of chefs in South Florida. Always pushing the boundaries of what is commonplace. Chef Allen brought evident stature to many foods unheard of until they became a part of his menus.

Norman Van Aken:
Cookery Bio:

Another legendary South Florida chef, **Norman Van Aken** is internationally known for his role in creating our New World Cuisine monarchy.

He is the only Floridian inducted into the prestigious *James Beard list of "Who's Who of Food and Beverage in America"* and was the winner of the coveted James Beard Award: "Best Chef in the Southeast".

He has been hailed as a *culinary genius* and has been given an honorary doctorate by Johnson and Wales University. He oversees several acclaimed restaurants rated "Best of" by Zagat. He has published four books: Feast of Sunlight *1988*, The Exotic Fruit Book *1995*, Norman's New World Cuisine *1997*, and New World Kitchen *2003*.

Weblink to Normans Cookbooks

BY RENOVATING HIS IDEALS ON WHAT NEW WORLD CUISINE COULD BE, HE CONTINUALLY INCORPORATES LOCAL LATINO HARVESTS INTO AN ALREADY VIBRANT TROPICAL CUISINE. BY MOVING TOWARDS MORE SPANISH CARIBBEAN FOOD ELEMENTS, NORMAN DEVELOPED A SPECIALIZED SEGMENT IN THIS SEGMENT OF A CUISINE.

LIKE OTHER CHEFS IN SOUTH FLORIDA, HIS CULTURE OF CUISINE IS DIVERGENT; IT IS NOW MORE COMFORT THAN CEREBRAL. BEING ON A PEDESTAL OF OUR CULINARY ZENITH FOR SO LONG ONE MIGHT WONDER WHY THE CHANGE FROM BEING IN THE FOREFRONT TO COMFORTABLY PEDESTRIAN. IT IS THE AWARENESS OF WHAT THE SOUTH FLORIDA CUSTOMER BASE NEEDS IN TODAY'S DINNING MARKETPLACE. IT IS NOT BEING EVERYTHING TO EVERYONE THAT IS THE WAY FOR THIS SOUTH FLORIDA CHEF; IT IS INSTEAD, BEING SPECIAL TO A SELECT CROWD THAT YOU ARE HAPPY TO CALL FRIENDS.

WEBLINK TO NORMAN VAN AKEN'S BLOG

CULINARY THOUGHT:

OF COURSE, HE IS AND HAS HE BEEN AN INNOVATOR FOR DECADES. HIS VIEWS ON FOOD AND THEIR PREPARATION HAS BECOME A LEGENDARY HALLMARK IN WHICH OTHER SOUTH FLORIDA CHEFS STRIVE TO REPLICATE. HE HAS ALWAYS ASTOUNDED ME WITH THE POETIC WORDING ON HIS MENUS, NARRATING HIS LOVE OF COOKING WITH TROPICAL FLAVORS. THE DESCRIPTIONS OF THE COMMONPLACE ARE PAIRED WITH THE EXOTIC MADE PLEASURABLE TO PERUSE.

COOKERY FINESSE:

CHEF NORMAN VAN AKEN'S FLAGSHIP EATERY IN MIAMI (NORMAN'S) - THOUGHT OF as a culinary Mecca for the wandering Avant Garde - was complemented by a triumphant gossamer of globally spanning culinary techniques, a deft hand with compelling flavors and accomplished cooking techniques. His new restaurant, filled with middling foods is braced with the culinary diplomacy of a global realization.

Production:

Norman's 360, his newest South Florida venture is uncomplicated with a robust feeling of enrichment after your meal. This chef's ideals are stroked through a powerful need to please others in common ways. It is the exotic products that are incorporated into his harmonizing menus that make this spot something of a local Tour-d'Force in Miami.

Cindy Hutson:
Cookery Bio:

Chef Cindy Hutson has urbanized a true to form Island-justification manner of cookery as she spins the traditional country-folk, rural cookery traditions of the Caribbean into a more metropolitan menu conception.

Chef Hutson is a self-taught chef who developed a passion for cooking at the age of nine. Inspired and amused by the television culinary genius of the "Galloping Gourmet" and Caribbean island-based "Chef Tell", she would mimic their T.V. creations in her own kitchen on Saturday afternoons.

Weblink to Chef Cindy Hutson's website

During her travels back and forth from Miami and the Blue Mountains of Jamaican, Hutson began cooking with an Island attitude. Each island stop helped her learn something about that island's saga and cuisine. As soon as she opened "Norma's on the Beach" in *1994*, it was touted as "the best Caribbean restaurant in South Florida" by publications such as USA Today, New York Times, London Times, Chicago Tribune, and Ocean Drive magazine.

She decided this original was a little too small so in *1999* she decided to move the original concept to a new location into the very "*tony*" Coral Gables. This new enhanced location came with a new name that earmarked the space as Caribbean leaning by naming it after the Jamaican citrus fruit "Ortanique". Chef Hutson flourished in her larger surroundings (120 seats) delving into South American, Asian, Caribbean, and American Fusion cuisine. Famed critic John Mariani, awarded it "Best New Restaurant 1999" Esquire Magazine.

As of late, she has opened another outpost on the new Caribbean culinary Mecca - Grand Cayman Island. Her new outpost on Grand Cayman is one of innovation and fun.

Thought:

Both Ortaniques restaurants have freed her to do guest chef appearances, teaching, and consulting. When asked "are you spreading yourself too thin?" Hutson replies "This culinary travel is what I thrive on, teaching other chef hopefuls about our earth's tropical bounties and edible history.

Finesse:

She loves to take the commonplace Caribbean foods and bring them into a Miami vogue. Removing some of the strings attached to a cuisine, she produces an earmarked culinary classic with a Flori-bbean jive.

Production:

Making use of South Florida's limitless bounty of tropical foods, she creates taste-variance wonders that astound all. Everything has a slant that cries Jamaican, yet a "down-home" consideration is remarkable.

DEWEY LOSASSO
COOKERY BIO:

As one of the founding members of the 1980's era "Mango Gang", a South Florida group of bold young chefs who put our fresh, tropical-accented cuisine on the culinary map. Chef Dewey LoSasso's growth as a ground breaking chef has not slowed since those heady days.

As a graduate of the Culinary Institute of America, he gravitated to South Florida in the early 1980's. He moved to the stewardship position of the Foundlings Club, an exclusive private membership club on Lincoln Road in Miami Beach. Here, Chef LoSasso began attracting discern for his creative, original cuisine, which he dubbed Florida Progressive. After a turn as Donatella Versace's personal chef and food event coordinator, Losso went to work for China Grill Manage-ment (CGM), serving as executive and concept chef for Tuscan Steak in Miami, and later relocating to New York.

WEBLINK TO AN INTERVIEW WITH CHEF DEWEY

Still under the aegis of the successful China Grill Management team, LoSasso then served as executive chef at New York's 950-room Hudson Hotel. After seven years in New York and the birth of two daughters, Dewey decided to cross the threshold into the Miami vista at the ultra-chic Forge restaurant on South Beach.

FINESSE:

His new digs have provided a culinary arena where he can experiment with the new and different. Here seemingly stale, haute cuisine is brought to new heights. Flavorful wallops from the tropical regions of the world govern the menu he has conceived here.

JAN JORGENSON:
COOKERY BIO:

The singular talent behind Two Chefs restaurant. Located in the heart of South Miami, Two Chefs is led by Chef Jorgenson, a classically trained chef whose inspired cuisine has made Two Chefs one of South Florida's sustained landmark restaurants.

Jorgenson fell in love with cooking at the age of 16, when he enjoyed a classic European apprenticeship. Upon graduating high school, he trained in some of the leading European cooking schools, eventually graduating with honors. Interested in a change of scenery, he moved to South Florida. Close to four years later and hearing of exciting new culinary trends in California, Jorgenson relocated to San Francisco, where he began working with Jeremiah Tower, one of the West Coast's vanguard culinary talents. Under Tower's tutelage, he sharpened his skills at Speedo 690 – one of the country's first Pacific Rim restaurants. Missing Miami, he returned and in 1992 to launch JanJo's in Coconut Grove. It was here that Jorgenson first drew the national spotlight, observance from prestigious national publications such as: Esquire, Travel + Leisure and Food & Wine. He developed his own South Florida leaning culinary style and in 1994, Jorgenson left JanJo's and launched Two Chefs in South Miami.

THOUGHT:

Bringing that *light* touch from the West Coast, he was able to create a noteworthy menu premise that changed as Miami's population changed. Chef Jan rode out the French Nouveau, the New World Cuisine, the new Latino and the Palm Tree cuisine fads and ultimately produces Miami's principally sought after menus.

PRODUCTION:

He produces a wide-ranging conglomerative cuisine wrapped up in a short list of ever-changing menu

SELECTIONS. HIS EUROPEAN EXECUTION AND PLATING PROFICIENCY WITH SOUTH FLORIDA'S FAVORITE SEAFOOD ENDOWS CHEF JAN ACCURATELY.

INTERVIEW WITH CHEF JAN JORGENSON

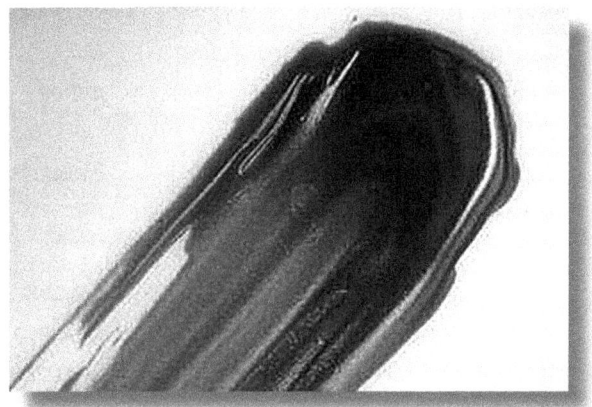

The Third Generation:

This new generation was brought up in the kitchens of our first South Floridian culinary leaders. They searched for their voice bringing in worldwide sourced foods and cooking techniques originating from around the tropical latitudes. Commonly known as *Palm Tree Cuisine*, they are the cookery ideals and thought apropos cooking techniques originating from the equatorial regions of the World-where *palm trees* grow.

This is where we lost our way towards a Florida-based cuisine that made sense. In the professional kitchen, it was like the 1970's counterculture all over again, if it feels good do it!

An important thing did happen, this new generation of chef started reaching back towards their roots. They bring with them the remnants of their family's cookery heritages and look backward to lay a pathway to our cookery future.

Andrea and Frank Randazzo: Cookery Bio:

Andrea, originally from Vero Beach, Florida was raised in an Italian family but, grew up in the halls of the Culinary Institute of America. Frank and Andrea found each other in this business, married and bring their children up in the business.

Weblink to an interview with Frank and Andrea Randanzzo

They highlight their careers working in Miami restaurants after both working in New York. Their menus feature an eclectic American cuisine that is inspired by their shared Italian-American heritage. Together they bring a little something classic to every new menu.

Thought:

Bringing together the flavors they adored by using what their parents taught them, Frank and Andrea have brought a new innovative meaning to the term multi-cultural cookery. Menus always nuanced by flavors from Asia and the Southwest. Once associated with the Pan-Asian culinary movement, now their menus parallel a voyage around the world.

Finesse:

The once Bravo Television star, Andrea and Frank Randanzzo bring to the table a reassurance that what you see on their menus is uppermost avant-garde. Each dish begins with high quality, fresh ingredients, cooked using a variety of classic techniques, with a jolt of flavor stemming from Mediterranean-Asian and Southwest. Their powerful cookery fusion excites with layered true and borrowed flavors.

Michael Bloise:

Cookery Bio:

Michael's French cuisine-based culinary training is accented with clean Asian vehemence all the while revisiting his Italian roots throughout a potpourri of South Florida influenced cuisine.

Michael is Italian-bred yet, Asian-tempered. In his childhood home the basis of family meals were scarce in proteins, and this gave way to the inevitability to cook via infinite boldness replicating his family's motherland.

As a graduate of Johnson and Wales University, Chef Michael's career broadened as he found ways to interact and exchange culinary ideals with his peers and mentors. Chef Frank Randazzo is one of those mentors that taught Michael how to realize his approach as a hotel chef. Chef Frank Randazzo also schooled Michael on the South Florida market that eventually led to lay the groundwork of how to find his menu skill that the customer can appreciate and respond to. "This is the ultimate achievement as a restaurateur", says Chef Michael. This tutelage escorted Michael to pilot **Wish**, a perennial favorite with local food critics. Chef Michael was able to resource lofty praise for **Wish** via deploying a fresh culinary savvy when he went back to his Italian roots to stylize this menu. Food economy schooling conveyed distinctly different and socialized cuisines into a conversant tropical realm.

Weblink to Michael Bloise interview

THOUGHT:

The flow of thought of this NEW wave chef is towards pleasures "to be experienced" and not towards conformity of any culinary consoling. Crowning his theory with this statement, he says: "If there were not a French Classical cuisine to base everything else on, there might not be a destiny for the new and different." He follows up with: "The rudiments of our modern culinary field have been learned throughout every chef's life and is the base upon which all other changes are supported." Meaning, that if there were not any culinary traditions, innovations might not follow because everything would have to be rediscovered each time a chef picks up a knife. Instead, it is our traditions that give us the ability to build upon and increase our new culinary distinctions.

Chef Michael's ideals of, "always making it better", is his idea of formulating a new cuisine. Michael has found that his Asian cookery background helped him bring an ever so slight culinary nuance onto his metropolitan stylized cuisine. An example is when Michael learned that with a dexterous hand, a slight bit of the Asian fish sauce brings depth to a classical cuisine-based sauce.

All his previous culinary mentors have framed a destiny for this chef. Once a director of many other chefs, he is now a director of communal sharing. He wants people to feel the comfort of his cooking and to share in the pleasure of effortless dining. To him, sharing in the customer's joy is his joie de vivre.

In his current culinary domicile, Michael communes more intimately with his clientele to a further extent than he did at his post at *Wish*. This one on one vibe is his now his joy of life. It is not one of grandiose culinary tradition; it is the family-oriented feeling and a personal approach that drives Chef Michael.

Michael's mother taught him a sense of economy and humility of cooking better without embellishments. This joy of simplicity brings forth a feeling of contentment.

It is taste, which drives this chef, no matter the tradition. This is what the "Culture of Cuisine" is all about.

Finesse:

Michael's earliest years drove him towards a life of upscale cuisine. After years as a premier cuisine merchant, he needed to go back to the roots of his life to produce simple gustatory pleasures. Cuisine is a personal journey for every chef. It is through the food that he conjures as an art medium that makes this chef unique.

Michael's mother taught that bold tastes makes one as fulfilled as over-stuffing oneself with a starch-laden meal. The finesse of assertive meals makes for a pleasure that is different, yet just as satisfying at the end of the day.

Production:

Food is the source of happiness. Its production is just the tool which we use to share this feeling of experimentation.

He found that being in an environment where he can pursue his art akin being in the home - cooking for his friends and family - was more his calling. He also found that the generosity of Asian ingredients that are grown here is amazing. South Florida is in the sub-tropical climate zone. Globally sourced tropically Asian foods transplanted here from around the tropical equator find their way onto menus varying from elementary to ambitious.

Our weather drives chefs to emphasize lightness of meals. Our chefs have learned that the basis of our culinary culture is keeping menus light but bold in flavors. Being flooded with starch-based meals is more acceptable by those who live north of the Mason-Dixon Line.

CUSTOMER BASE MOST LIKELY DETERMINES THE SUCCESS OF A CUISINE. THE EVIDENCE OF PORTABILITY OF OUR CULTURE OF CUISINE IS A LARGE CONCERN. THE WAY THAT FOOD IS ROUTINELY SHIPPED FROM ALL POINTS OF THE GLOBE, WITH THE RIGHT CUSTOMER BASE, THIS CULINARY CULTURE WILL BE RELEVANT IN ANY AREA OF THE COUNTRY.

A CHEF'S MENU BESPEAKS OF THE FOOD'S ORIGINS. MANY TIMES IN A CULINARY CULTURE, THERE IS AN UNIFYING INGREDIENT. IN OUR SOUTH FLORIDA CULTURE, IT HAS TO BE THE MANGO. AFTER DECADES OF COMMON USE IN SOUTH FLORIDA, RESTAURANTS AROUND THE WORLD NOW USE THE "*KING OF FRUIT*". "SO COMMONLY USED HERE, THAT APPLES AND ORANGES SEEM WEARISOME." THROUGHOUT THE ASIAN-GLOBAL CUISINE, TROPICAL FOODS SUCH AS MANGOS ARE AN EGREGIOUS CULINARY COMPONENT.

THIS CHEF HAS FILTERED THE CULTURE OF SOUTH FLORIDA CUISINE THROUGH THE *CHINOSE* OF GLOBAL POSTURE TO FORMULATE HIS OWN SOUTH FLORIDA STYLE.

CHRIS NORTON
CULINARY BIO:

TRAINED WITH PREMIER DINING ROOM CHEFS, EARLIER IN HIS CAREER CHEF CHRIS WAS A LUXURY YACHT AND CRUISE SHIP CHEF. HIS TENURE OF MORE THAN 20 YEARS AT FORT LAUDERDALE'S PREMIER BEACHFRONT RESTAURANT, *ARUBA BEACH CAFE'S* CHEF CHRIS MIGHT BE SYMBOLIC OF A TYPICAL BEACH CHEF.

AN UNEQUALED BEACH FRONT RESTAURANT, ITS STATURE AND THE VIEWS ARE ABOVE COMPARE. IT IS A TRUE SOUTH FLORIDA DINING LANDMARK. CHEF CHRIS HAS LED ARUBA BEACH CAFE TO NUMEROUS ACCOLADES DURING HIS TWO DECADES LONG STINT. THE RESTAURANT HAS SEEN ITS GROWING PAINS BUT NOW CRUISES ALONG AS SMOOTHLY AS THE SUNRISE STRETCHES ACROSS THE HORIZON.

WEBLINK TO CHEF CHRIS WEBSITE

THOUGHT:

Make the typical seafood dishes eye-catching. Chris' menu is customer friendly. There is something here for anyone. Seafood of course is the main culinary objective.

When it comes to running a restaurant, Chris does it right. The seats, all 300 of them, are always full even on weekdays. The restaurant is a local hangout and attracts tourists like no other place along the Strand. Chef Chris has found after two decades of giving people what they want, they will always come back. Easy thought process right? I have found in my thirty years of cooking in and around South Florida, that this concept is lost to many restaurateurs.

FINESSE:

Overflowing with years of classical cuisine cookery behind him, Chef Chris has found how to adapt towards Florida's lighter (cuisine) side. He has taken the classic seafood Steamer-pot and made it anew. When this dish comes to your table, you are looking for some friends to help you eat it.

"Classic cookery is what drives all of our new menu items", says the chef. He continues, "If it was not for the basis of classic cookery, we would have nowhere to start from." This is what we see every day in South Florida. Chefs using their years of honed cookery skills in French or Italian classic cookery to reshape the new ideas.

PRODUCTION:

The kitchen is amazingly small here for accomplishing the sales in the tens of millions. "We have an old fashion beach-pit Pig roast on the weekends that gets our locals here", says the chef. Again, he has built his business on what the customers perceive as an experience and a value.

LINDA GASSENHEIMER

I appreciate another author's point of view on these topics. Linda has been a great source of inspiration for many South Floridian chefs and home cooks alike.

AUTHOR BIO:

WEBLINK TO LINDA'S COOKBOOK WEBSITE

Linda Gassenheimer is a South Florida based culinary personality that has earned her share of journalistic related kudos.

As a noted cookbook author and weekly syndicated food columnist, she writes a widely distributed column read by over six million readers.

Linda enjoys her role as a liaison between the formally trained culinary professional and the homemaker. She says: "It keeps me in touch with professional chefs and where I translate your experiences to create meals people want to make at home." Her recipes are easy to make, good for you and, most important of all, have great taste.

Linda produces and hosts a weekly segment, "Food News and Views", on WLRN National Public Radio and makes many guest appearances on numerous radio and television programs throughout the United States and Canada.

THOUGHT:

Linda has seen trends come and go in South Florida. The best trend in her eyes as of late is the fresh from the farm idea. Chefs are producing menus that use only local farm raised ingredients in their menus.

Local farmers from the Redlands in the south, north to West Palm Beach and west over to Lake Okeecobee are all producing the foods that are being highlighted in today's modern menus.

Linda points out the fact that her training at Le Cordon Bleu in Europe stressed this many years ago. While overseas, she began her love affair for food and writing about the cooking she experienced while living there. After writing three books: "French Cuisine", "Simply Sauces" and "Italian Cuisine", she became enthralled with South Florida and the foods she discovered here. One of her most recent books, "Keys Cuisine", depicts what a laid-back place South Florida is. It is filled with the new and different. The newly released cookbook "Keys" tells of what it is like to dine and experience foods from numerous iniquitous restaurants across Key West.

Finesse:

Linda exemplifies South Florida home cooking with her writing. Always being in contact with local South Floridian readers, she knows about the "Soul" of our cookery heritage. She believes that homey feeling of food cooked the way Grandma did, down to earth and naturally good for you, is the basis of most Miamian home cooking. No matter the heritage, it is the old ways (referring to cookery) that keeps the family happy. In her own family, they are the new recipe testers and when she brings a new dish to the table for evaluation, there is always applause for the classics. Not playing with their placement on the plate or, tedious presentations, just effortless cookery virtue. They are the dishes that look like they are just what they are meant to be.

She has noted that the best restaurants in town are the ones with time tested foods and locally sourced favorites.

A CHEF ALWAYS TRIES TO SOURCE LOCAL PRODUCTS THAT ARE FREQUENTLY A FRESHER PRODUCT AND IN MOST CIRCUMSTANCES, IT IS ALSO A HEALTHY COOKING OPTION. LOCALLY SOURCED FOODS PREDOMINANTLY RAISED ORGANICALLY VAUNT THE TASTE THAT SHOUTS "*SOUL OF THE EARTH*". CREATING RECIPES THAT SPEAK FOR THEMSELVES IS THE WAY SHE APPOINTS NEW TASTES TO A DINER. SHE LOVES THE HOGFISH RECIPE IN HER NEW COOKBOOK. IT IS COOKED AND SAUCED WITH AN EFFORTLESS COMBINATION OF TOMATO, GARLIC, MANGO PUREE AND CHIVES. THE SWEETNESS OF THE MANGO PUREE COUNTERACTS THE SOMETIMES ACIDIC TOMATO AND EVERYTHING JUST WORKS TOGETHER AS A NATURAL BALANCE OF COMPOSURE.

SHE LOVES THE SMACK AND THE SOULFUL EXPOSURE IN RENDITIONS OF SWEET AND SAVORY. THE MINGLING OF MANGO WITH THE SAVORY ELEMENTS OF CUMIN AND CORIANDER IN A PORK RECIPE CAN BE A HIGHLIGHT FOR ANY KITCHEN. SHE CREDITS THE ENGLISH COLONISTS FOR BEING SO BOLD AS TO EXPERIMENT WITH SO MANY TASTES FROM AROUND THE GLOBE. SHE NOTES THAT NOW IN ENGLAND THE SMELL OF CURRY DISHES FILL THE STREETS WHERE THE AROMA OF MINCEMEAT PIES ONCE SETTLED. LINDA OBSERVED THAT NOT ONLY THE ENGLISH BUT ALSO THE FRENCH ARE ON BOARD. "YOU WOULD HAVE SEEN ASIAN COOKING ELEMENTS IN A FRENCH RESTAURANT TWENTY YEARS AGO". LINDA HAS NOTED THAT EVEN THE EMINENT EUROPEAN CHEFS HAVE MELIORATED THEIR OWN CULINARY INFLUENCES CULLING FROM OUR TROPICAL UNIVERSE AND IT HAS AFFECTED THE ARCHETYPICAL STYLE AND VOICE IN THE EUROPEAN FINALISTIC ARENA.

ALICE WEINGARTEN

COOKERY BIO:

THE FOOD REVOLUTION OF THE '70S COINCIDED WITH CHEF ALICE WEINGARTEN'S COMING OF AGE IN THE NORTHERN LATITUDES WHERE SHE LIVED. AFTER MANY YEARS OF FAMILY BASED COOKERY TRAINING, SHE FOUND HERSELF AS ONE OF ONLY A FEW FEMALE STUDENTS AT THE VENERABLE *CULINARY INSTITUTE OF AMERICA* IN HYDE PARK, NEW YORK.

Celebrated Florida chef Alice Weingarten was already well versed in the art of food at the age of fifteen-and-a-half: her mother always kept a two-pound tin of Beluga in the fridge. At 17, she published her carrot cake recipe in Gourmet magazine, pursuing formal training at the venerable Culinary Institute of America seemed the logical next step.

It is clear that Alice imparts her personal philosophy through her food, which is at once comforting, delectable and beautiful. In Key West, Alice has found a home for her distinctive cooking style.

Thoughts:
Alice has a personal philosophy about food that decrees that it should be — among other things — comforting. Her cuisine itself bespeaks of her other beliefs that it should be delicious, beautiful to look at, and composed of a variety of flavors and textures. Alice's food is described as a mix of whimsical Asian, Mediterranean, Cuban and Caribbean creations with her mother's meat loaf thrown in for good measure.

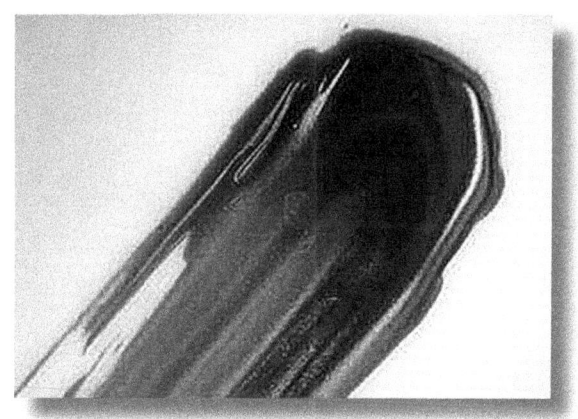

CHAPTER SIX

YOU AND YOUR CULINARY FUTURE:

WHAT EVERY CHEF AND RESTAURATEUR SHOULD KNOW BEFORE CREATING A SOCIAL PRESENCE.

SOCIAL MEDIA AND WHAT IT MEANS TO YOU!

THERE IS A SECRET WEAPON FOR THE FUTURE OF THE RESTAURANT BUSINESS SUCCESSES ~SOCIAL MEDIA~ THE INTERNET IS YOUR MEDIA OUTREACH TOOL!

CHEF MICHAEL BENNETT'S
WEB BLOG

CHEF MICHAEL BENNETT
WRITING IN TORTOLA, BVI

This topic is as varied as it is broad. Everything that I could write about here has and will change by the time you read this. The 'Net changes fast and to keep up is basically a full-time job.

The proliferation of Internet based social media sites has grown since I started to write this book.

Social media is the new promotional tool for chefs. Using the obliging and ubiquitous social media avenues, you are able to tell your story to current and future customers for very little. Again, it is as much a curse as it is a cure. I follow the blogs, the posts from the new leaders in this field and I will tell you, it takes time. This is the curse. The cure is the ability to reach people around the world without hiring an expensive PR firm.

Social media channels are varied. There are many new Internet media companies out there. Some are reliable

some, are not. The social media sites that you "have to" belong to are: Facebook, Myspace, Wordpress, AOL's "Lifestream", Yahoo's companies like: Buzz, Flickr and Shine, Google's companies like: YouTube, Blogspot, GoogleMaps and Buzz, Twitter, Twaitter, Tumblr, Ping, FOURsquare, StumbleUpon, LinkedIn, Readdit, Yammer, Meetup and Ning, Fishbowl, Yelp....and each of these companies will change in significance on a daily basis.

You as a chef have to keep these media outlets at the top of your mind when considering communication options to customers. Maybe it is not a daily chore for you yet but, you need to make someone in your company responsible for activating and maintaining these communication outlets. It is common for a restaurant to have a paid staffer do social media updates. You should always choose the fresh, hip dude or dudette to make pertinent additions to your social media systems. The job is a full time one, in the beginning of your restaurant you might need to hire and keep multiple social media staffers. One person should be responsible for conception of the medium and a another person should work to make sure it all gets pitched and placed to the right playing field.

Becoming More Social:

Restaurant marketers that are early in their social media marketing maturity level tend to focus on message distribution such as Tweeting or posting Facebook links mostly to their own content vs. engaging with customers on a human level.

That old style "one-way" communication profile (similar to placing an advertisement in the local newspaper) doesn't bring forth one-on-one discussions and information sharing, so social media viewership and flow of communication traffic levels tend to dull early and page views tend to diminish.

To heighten the benefit of social media marketing investments, your staff needs to foresee and facilitate more on being "social" rather than on "marketing".

Here are some tips on how to proceed:

Decide what you stand for topically and this will authorize your *Ideals* to mesh with what the restaurant needs. What is your niche? Are you a seafood house or a natural food, gluten-free or whatever the trend of the moment is eatery?

Keyword Load everything.

The social Search Engine Optimization benefits of being deliberate with your wordsmithing is where you need to highlight your key business model. Focus on the "*social*" of the Social Media conversations happening within your target community. Don't let your voice be topically fragmented. Keyword optimizing of your Blogs and Social

NETWORKING CONTENT DONE WRONG CAN DILUTE A COMPANY'S ABILITY TO "STAND OUT" AND DEMONSTRATE A MATURE VISION TO THEIR CUSTOMERS.

YOUR GOAL FOR ANY SOCIAL INTEGRATION SHOULD BE TO LAY OUT A STRATEGY THAT CLASSIFIES YOUR MEASURABLE IMPROVEMENT GOALS, ATTEMPTING TO CULTIVATE (CUSTOMER-RELATED) PERSONAS AND READABLE CONTENT GEARED TOWARDS WHO YOUR CUSTOMER IS. CONTENT SET FOR A WOMAN SHOULD NOT BE THE SAME WRITTEN WORDS THAT YOU SHOULD ADD TO YOUR BLOGS AND MEDIA CONTENT FOR MEN.

CONTENT (YOUR WRITTEN WORDS) STRATEGY HAS TO BE EXECUTED AND SHOULD DEMONSTRATE YOUR IDEALS AND TO PROMOTE YOUR BRAND LABEL. IT SHOULD FLAVOR SOCIAL NETWORK DISCOURSE GEARED SPECIFICALLY TOWARDS THE DISPOSITION OF YOUR READERSHIP. CREATE INTERESTING CONTENT FOR YOUR READERSHIP TO RESPOND TO BY THE FLAVOR THAT YOU ARE LEADING YOUR READERS

TO TASTE. CREATE TOPICS OF FOCUS THAT WILL INTEREST THE READERS TO CONTINUE TO READ ON AND THROUGH THIS CONTENT MASSAGING, IT WILL ELEVATE YOU AS A LEADER IN THIS PROCESS.

USE KEY TOPIC FOCUS TO DRAW EYES TO YOUR CONTENT. PARTICIPATE WITH YOUR CUSTOMERS IN A CONVERSATIONAL TONE. FIND WHERE AND HOW THEY SPEND THEIR TIME AND THEN FOCUS ONTO THESE ARENAS. CREATE USEFUL CONTENT THAT THEY CAN USE IN THEIR LIVES AND TELL OF HOW YOU HAVE A COMMANDING EDGE ON THE TOPIC. MAKE SURE EVERYTHING YOU CREATE AND PROMOTE IS THOUGHTFUL AND FITS IN YOUR *SOCIAL & CONTENT MARKETING PLAN*.

IT MEANS THE UPSHOT OF YOUR EFFORTS IS THE INVOLVEMENT THAT YOU HAVE CREATED IS YOUR OWN. READERSHIP CAN BE MOLDED WHICHEVER WAY BENEFITS YOU FOR THE GREATEST RETURNS. THESE DISCUSSIONS WILL BUILD YOUR BRAND AS THESE INTERACTIONS ARE CULTIVATED. AS YOUR TARGET AUDIENCE SEES AND REACTS TO THIS BRAND-BUILDING, YOU WILL BECOME known as an expert in this line of communication and on the topics discussed.

Design a Win-Win:

Plan your efforts without comprising your bottom line. Your efforts won't see dramatic returns until gradual deletion of printed media is removed from your P&L. Plan on covering the basics: Facebook, Linked In, Twitter, Google, etc...then go beyond your comfort zone to integrate into localized blogs and websites that create different city-wide social interests. Working in this mode is like a giant networking meeting where you do not know anyone at first but then by the end of the meeting you had met three new friends. Your content should inspire readers to interact and be a part of your community. Say something proactive. It at first draws eyes then viewership loyalty because everyone wants to be a part of something on the cutting edge. As you find your niche, train others in your organization to mimic your style as they begin to create their own personas while expanding your brand.

This also means that in your P&L forecasts, you will plan on lowering the investment dedicated to print media and spend a little more on acquiring people's social engagement through setup and perpetual costs that help you allocate and expand your brand.

Do a forecast on what you think it will take to reimburse people for sharing their experiences on line with you. It can be as easy as asking people who come to your place to write something on *Yelp.com* or "like" your *Facebook* page. Sometimes the best incentive is to give them food while they are at your restaurant. Food cost being 1/3 of the value perceived by the customer goes a long way to stretch those marketing dollars. Test your results of increased volume in hits to your websites, blogs, FB "likes",

TWITTER SIGN UPS, ETC... AS YOU TEST AND RECORD WHAT WORKS, REPEAT IT NEVER FORGETTING IT IS YOUR INTERACTION THAT DRAWS MORE INTERACTION FROM THE READERSHIP. YOUR ENGAGEMENT IN ONE ARENA WILL MOST LIKELY EXPAND TO OTHER ARENAS COMPELLING YOU TO ADD MORE PEOPLE TO POST AND REPLY TO THESE NEW SEGMENTS OF YOUR SOCIAL NETWORK.

INCREASING SALES ARE EASILY MEASURED WHEN YOU KNOW WHAT TO LOOK FOR. DEVISE A TRIGGER INSTRUMENT THAT HELPS YOU SEE THE NEW INVOLVEMENT LIKE: "SIGNUP FOR OUR NEWSLETTER" OR "'LIKE US' ON FACEBOOK AND RECEIVE YOUR FIRST COCKTAIL ON US". NOT ONLY DOES THE FREE COCKTAIL IMPLY THAT YOU ARE REQUIRED TO BUY ANOTHER ONE, MOST RESTAURANTS RUN A 10% COST ON PERCEIVED VALUE OF THIS ITEM. WHEN YOU DOMINATE THIS SOCIAL MEDIA TERRITORY, COMPARED TO YOUR COMPETITION, YOU WILL SEE HIGHER QUALITY RESULTS MAGNIFIED EACH AND EVERY TIME YOU MAKE NEW CUSTOMER CONNECTIONS.

SEO FASHIONING....

WHEN YOU OPTIMIZE YOUR SOCIAL MEDIA CONTENT FOR BETTER HITS FROM SEARCH ENGINES, IT IS NOT THE SAME AS PROBING FOR CUSTOMERS WITH ADVERTISING. MARKETING IS ONE THING SEO (SEARCH ENGINE OPTIMIZATION) IS ANOTHER.

YOU WANT TO GET TO THE TOP OF ANY SEARCH ENGINE'S LIST OF SEARCHED TOPICS. LET'S SAY YOUR CUSTOMER IS SEARCHING FOR "RESTAURANTS IN SOUTH FLORIDA", YOU HAVE TO HAVE THE ACTUAL WORDS "*SOUTH FLORIDA AND RESTAURANT*" IN THE CONTENT OF YOUR PAGES OR THE SEARCH ENGINES WILL NOT RANK YOUR PAGES HIGH ENOUGH FOR YOUR CUSTOMERS TO SEE THEM. WORDS THAT REFER TO SOUTH FLORIDA OR RESTAURANT WON'T WORK. IT IS BEST TO HAVE YOUR TOPIC WORDS IN THE TITLE,

HEADING OF THE BLOG OR WEBPAGE AND IN THE FIRST PARAGRAPH ABOUT 3-5 TIMES. IN THE REST OF CONTENT "BODY" OF THE PAGES, YOU NEED TO HAVE IT IN THE "BODY" ANOTHER TWO TO THREE TIMES. THIS IS *KEYWORD LOADING* AND IT IS HOW SEARCH ENGINES WILL MEASURE YOUR PAGES FOR RELEVANCY. IF YOUR CHOSEN KEYWORDS ARE IN THE COPY SEVERAL TIMES THROUGH THE ENTIRE SITE, THE SEARCH ENGINES WILL RECOGNIZE THIS PAGE AS RELEVANT TO THE SEARCH CRITERIA THAT YOUR CUSTOMER IS SEARCHING FOR AND PLACE IT IN FRONT OF THE READER FIRST (OR HIGHER UP) ON HIS COMPUTER. THIS IS A VERY TEDIOUS TOPIC AND ONE THAT YOU MIGHT WANT TO FARM OUT TO YOUR MORE "HIP" COMPUTER GEEK EMPLOYEES.

A NOTE:

89% OF ALL PEOPLE WHO DINE FIRST RESEARCH WHERE THEY ARE GOING TO EAT ONLINE! THIS IS ESPECIALLY TRUE IN TOURISTS BASED LOCATIONS. YOU HAVE TO KNOW WHAT YOUR CUSTOMERS ARE LOOKING FOR AND PROVIDE THEM *VALUE.*

KNOW AND UNDERSTAND TRENDS.

COMMUNICATE WITH AND TO THE RIGHT PEOPLE! MARKETING NOWADAYS IS A CONVERSATION BETWEEN YOU AND YOUR CUSTOMERS. NOT JUST SHOUTING OUT AN ADVERTISING MESSAGE AND HOPING SOMEONE WILL BE THERE TO READ IT OR HEAR IT. *ENGAGE THEM*!

KEY IDEAS ON A SOCIAL MEDIA RICH LIFE

- YOU DO NOT NEED TO BE A TECHIE TO ACCOMPLISH A LOT. KNOW YOUR CUSTOMERS AND MEET THEIR NEEDS. TWO-THIRDS OF TRAVELERS USE THE WEB EXCLUSIVELY TO PLAN TRAVEL.

- CONSIDER THE BEST POSSIBLE MEASURES FOR YOUR MARKETING SUCCESS. THEN MEASURE IT FOR SUCCESS. MOST OF US MEASURE RESULTS LIKE PHONE CALLS AND EMAILS IN RESPONSE TO YOUR MARKETING EFFORTS.

- CONSIDER *YOUR WEBSITE* AS THE *CENTER* OF ALL YOUR MEDIA. MEANING: ALWAYS POST GOOD NEWS, TEXT RESPONSES to published articles, and publish all video and photos from your customers on dedicated pages in your website. If you give anyone the ability to post these FREE you will see more interaction with your guests. When distribution is free, reallocate distribution expenses to production of stories.

- Travelers want your photos so make them downloadable. Also, give your webpage visitors the opportunity to load their own pictures to your site. There are over two billion picture uploads per month on Facebook. Flickr is at 90 million per month. So it would be a good start for your Facebook page to have uploadable capabilities. Facebook is adding *half a million new users every day*. Don't you think some of them are your ideal guests?

- Position your social media contact points in obvious places in print media: i.e. – printed restaurant receipts, restaurant and personal business cards, advertising posters and any distributed brochures.

Over 44% of all Internet users are active in social media.

- 19% of travelers visit blogs before going on vacation.
- 1/3 of all users have written a review after their trip.
- 42% upload movies to YouTube.
- 33% use Facebook to show pictures of their trip.
- 27% of most travelers use Trip Advisor
- 73% of travelers search for photos before they travel to a place.

- Twitter: 60 million users and a 1171% growth rate. Worth getting in? Who hasn't used this immediate response device? The best thing for businesses is that Twitter provides common answers to quick questions from customers. I think everyone that is reading this book knows what to do here.

- Social Media is not optional. Your business is naked. The biggest shift in investment needs to succeed in social media is from money to time. Where are you going to find the time to do the most important things? Everyone has an audience. 59 percent think customer reviews are more important than professional reviews. 63 percent are more likely to purchase if a company has reviews.

Deadly Sins of Social Media...
Sinful efforts include:
- Thinking you can control it. Once it is on the 'Net it is there forever.

- Being unprepared for negatives. Use each question of quality as an opportunity to increase your visibility in fixing the problem.

- Taking time to respond, see above on this reasoning.... Slow responses mean you don't care or are unaware and that could be the death knell to the Internet savvy crowd.

Being deaf to conversation that includes your brand, region, and your services will deter your visits from the largely aware Internet savvy crowd.

Do not think your reputation rests with management. You do and can change the way people think about you while you comment and post to FaceBook.

- Expecting others to protect your brand and the right business blog or Facebook Fan page is a critical error. The right message can increase revenue 20%.

- Charging for Internet access. Give Away WiFi access and never stop asking for faster wired & handheld

Internet access in your community. High speed Internet access can double the revenue generating capacity across all industries in communities without it. Faster / better speeds will likely increase revenue.

Do – Do these things!

- Do position your real world contact points in obvious places: newspaper and magazine advertisements, brochures, online marketing including your phone number and email address on everything. Handheld smartphone users can click on to the contact information and it will connect you immediately.

- Over 90% of cell phone users have their phones with them 24/7.

- 60% of the people in world have cell phone contracts (3.1 billion). Phones are replaced every 18 months. Most new phones are smartphones. This will be the Web marketing channel that matters most in travel.

- Ask your fans to tell their story on TripAdvisor and embed a link in emails, tag lines, websites and business cards. The real goal of your business is not to make sales through your postings to Facebook, et.al, it is to create FANS.

- Current'cy is the new Currency. Be aware what is going on around you. In the community and what your customers care about.

- Check your listing on Google Maps. It is like free yellow pages. The Here and Now Web means all your digital assets should be linked to a location.

39% of North Americans now have smart phones, double from 2008. 35% of 8 year olds in the U.K. have cell phones. Don't you think it is about time to place advertising in the right place?

Shop and pay with your phone?

- **Smartphone Apps** are here to stay. Starbucks is leading the way. Their *app* for smartphones is now recognized worldwide. You use it like a credit card in your wallet. Instead of opening your wallet and sliding the card through the machine, you just let the laser reader read your smartphone screen and money is taken from the preloaded account.

Your app should be able to...

- Provide links to all your social media - use QR codes.

- Allow fans to purchase directly from their phone or handheld device like Starbucks does.

- Allow your fans to upload and share their stories across all media types.

- Allow your fans to make reservations directly through their smartphones.

- Allow them to participate in common holiday events via your restaurant networking online.

- It must be easily accessible and easily remembered. Make the app and its location on the internet easy to find.

Example: Hilton watched handheld revenue only double from mobile site year over year 2008-2009. Then in May, month to month handheld sales started soaring! Up 400% month over month from May to October.

- Maybe you need to shift some of your print advertising budget to app development.

- Thinking app: *Think* iPhone, Blackberry, Android... in that order. The amount of people using these products will and do change from time to time but at this moment in history these are the big three.

- Collaborate with others in your community to install a restaurant "*Cloud*" resource that travelers can access to see valuable and timely information about your restaurant and its services. Or... banquets, part planning, to-go preplanning for rushed lunch hour workers, etc...

- Hire for skills in production and social media distribution. Think beyond traditional job descriptions and application forms. Add some social media

questions like: Which Web sites do you use?

Restaurant marketing using QR codes and the Internet

- QR Codes - in Japan readers are on 70% of new phones and can hyperlink to any place or object on the Web.

QR Codes and your Smartphone.

- Both use the internet equally well to perform delivering your promotions. Smartphone usage is so popular now it is strange not to see a teenager without one growing out of their hand. Estimates say that there are 73.3 million U.S. smartphone users in 2011, and 44% of them use their phone to surf the 'Net.

Quick Response codes (QR codes) read like bar codes when scanned by your smartphone and automatically send your phone to where the symbol is programmed to go. It could be a URL (or Web address) or business-card information or even a discount offer. I have seen them being used on business cards, email closing statements, brochures, billboards, magazine ads, car sales information stickers, trade show booths, explanatory signs for items of interests during a walking tour, contests and more.

Capture the interest of your smartphone using customers right now.

In your restaurant you surely have customers who use smartphones as a way of life. You might actually find them checking in to your establishment on Foursquare, Facebook or Gowalla (soon to be taken over by FourSquare). All use real-time location based technology and can better enhance the ability of new customers to find you in a sea of non-tech savvy entrepreneurs.

You can capture this fascination for apps and smartphones using QR code technology by making sure you follow these tips:

- Since most restaurants spend an absoradent amount of advertising dollars to find new customers, QR codes will help you retain current customers and make it easier for them to place a secondary order. All your carry-out menus should have the QR symbol on them. Make it easy to find, so that it is easier to use your direct contact information which is loaded onto their phones right then and there.

Make it fun for them to order again with their phones without dialing. Your phone number and other contact information should be the first symbol. The QR code will enable the user to dial your restaurant directly to make it easier to place a second order that week. Other ideas are to stack codes on the take-out materials so it is fun to use the brochure like a phone book of the internet. Just describe what each one will do as the customer uses it by highlighting and describing each icon, i.e...*go to your blog, website or your advertorial movie on YouTube.*

- Your business cards should have a scanable symbol on them. Think! - refrigerator door magnet business cards. If they take your card and put it on the refrigerator, they do not even have to use the phone book to find or dial a number to order their next pizza. Add a QR code on the back of a business card. This way, the first time the user scans your card, your address and complete contact information will be stored on their smartphone contact list.

- QR code linking to your menu photos. If you have pictures as part of menus or brochures place the QR symbol near the printed information so they can link to a recipe or a YouTube video on how the dish is made.

- Making your own repeat business coupons. Bringing back repeat business is always easier and cheaper on your marketing budget. Use the QR code to give the current patrons a discount on their next purchase.

- Use QR codes as a linking device to your Facebook page and give them a reason to "like" you there. Once a customer presses that button, you can continually send them blurbs about how your business is going and what they might expect the next time they arrive. Use QR codes to continually engage your customers and encourage them to join the fun on your Facebook page. Always make it worth their while to do so by giving them a *Club* membership-like offer. The membership might be as simple as first reservations for prime seating during holidays at your restaurant.

THE BIG BOYS OF THE INTERNET:

FOURSQUARE IS VIRAL ADVANTAGE. FOURSQUARE IS ONE OF THOSE NEW COMPANIES THAT WILL DO A BETTER MARKETING JOB FOR YOU IN THE FUTURE. IT IS A GEO-LOCATION SERVICE THAT DEALS WITH PEOPLE USING CELL PHONES TO TELL OTHER PEOPLE WHERE THEY ARE BY BLOGGING FROM. IT IS LIKE A GAME. BE PROACTIVE AND GET THEM TO TELL YOUR STORY TO OTHERS BY GIVING THEM SOMETHING BACK. THEIR BUSINESS MODEL IS TO GIVE USERS AWARDS IN THE FORM OF BADGES FOR SIGNING IN (AT THEIR CURRENT LOCATION) AND AS THEY CHECK IN OVER AND OVER AGAIN FROM A SINGLE LOCATION, THEY ARE ELIGIBLE TO BECOME THE "MAYOR" OF A CERTAIN LOCATION IF THEY GO THERE ENOUGH. YOU CAN AND SHOULD OFFER DEALS AND COUPONS TO THEM BECAUSE THEY ARE IN YOUR PLACE AT A CERTAIN TIME OF DAY, OR THEY VISIT A LOT AND TELL THEIR FRIENDS THEY ARE VISITING YOUR PLACE. USE THIS SERVICE

LIKE A *SPECIAL CLUB LEVEL* GIFT FOR ATTENDANCE AT YOUR PLACE.

FACEBOOK IS A GEO-BASED, PERSONAL INFORMATIONAL SHARING DEVICE THAT IS PLANNING TO BE EVERYTHING TO EVERYONE. THEIR BUSINESS MODEL IS TO COMPETE WITH GOOGLE'S GMAIL EMAILING SERVICE AND THIS WILL PLACE FACEBOOK AS THE MOST IMPORTANT TOOL IN YOUR BOX OF YOUR SOCIAL MEDIA UTENSILS.

TO START USING THIS COURSE YOU NEED TO CLAIM YOUR SPOT ON FACEBOOK PER A SOCIAL MEDIA PERSONALITY. MEANING: BUILD A DIFFERENT WEBPAGE AND PERSONALITY FOR EACH PART OF YOUR MEDIA STRATEGY. YOU SHOULD ALWAYS HAVE DIFFERENT WEBPAGE PERSONALITY FOR SALES AND ANOTHER PAGE FOR INFORMATION SHARING. YOUR INFORMATION-SHARING PAGE SHOULD BE BUILT BY THE YOUNG HIPSTER ON YOUR STAFF, TO KEEP THE FLOWING INFORMATION IN A FORMAT THAT IS ENTERTAINING AS WELL AS "KOOL".

This is what the social media game will look like for a while. But, there are other tools that should be in your box.

SOURCING INFORMATIONAL SITES:

The future of Social Media is not written yet! Information is not as important as the customer that is interacting with the information. Bloggers are important to filling in information being searched. 86% people who use this information will direct people to your site, information page, data source, phone number, address or GEO-position.

REAL-TIME MEDIA LIVE MEDIA MARKETING!

Feedly is a Google company. Being collective distributors as Feedly is, it collects information and distributes to people requesting content on a subject. An example is setting up a R.S.S. feed from someone's website. This is how *Google Reader* program works.

Their business model updates information automatically to your device as you request it to your own reader for consumption.

Your initiative should be to place content that is interesting about you and your restaurant on the internet. Base its vocabulary structuring upon specific *keyword* descriptions and thus keyword load all uploaded content.

Use wordsmiths (creative writers) to create the right content for you and your restaurant, remembering to "*keyword load*" and read well at the same time.

FULFILMENT OPTIONS:

AUGMENTED REALITY: business model is when these companies overlay pictures, videos and information overtop each other process on GEO-location devices and apps.

Example of this would be to load pictures of the

front of the restaurant (or menu items) atop **Foursquare's** reviews, mayor badges, etc...

Google and Adwords:

A specialized way of thinking about promoting your restaurant from your promotional advertising/ marketing verbiage. *Their business model offers:*

- 2.18 billion people use Google every day. Over 200K per hour.

- 100 % of new restaurant customers do research online.

- 90 % of growth in restaurants is happening through GOOGLE.

- Eight out of ten people use the internet.

- Nine out of ten (of these people) find info about restaurants online.

- 70 % (of these people) base their decisions upon what they see on the internet.

- 50 % of people are looking for offers or coupons.

- 40 % are looking for locations (Google's Maps).

- 30 % are looking for take-out foods.

- 45 % of all dining decisions are made by Mom.

- *So structure all content to what a Mom needs.*

- There is a 3-5 second decision window per page view. So keep content to the point and well written.

- ZERO second decision window = search engine keywords. Keyword loading is the most important thing to do. The correct Keywords will bring you the best page ranking results.

- 35 % of people decide what or where they go to eat at work during business hours.

- 28 % make last second decisions – *phone*

based decisions. And, there has been a 59% growth in mobile devices.

- Top ten searches across the Internet are restaurant searches.

- Eight millions video searches are about restaurants.

- Brand a YouTube channel about your place to increase views. To succeed you have to be:

    o Visible,-see above facts and comments below

- Persuasive, - know what your customers want and provide it to them.

- Flexible – Virally promote.

- Be proactive. Keep them engaged and wanting more.

- Send reminders about special events in or out of house.

- Keep communications open and constant all year.

- Keep all conversations interesting, funny, informational, etc…create a buzz and keep it at the *"Top of the Mind"* by diners with constant contacts from you. Make all your conversations memorable!

- And, of course, your own email and newsletters.

Just like a listing of friends, that you send personal notes to, you should have your list of media people that you have on your email/newsletter speed dial.

Having a well-written newsletter that is emailed every month to your customer base is an imperative necessity.

Newsletters can keep you at the top of the customer's mind. Do not forget to structure your content to the viewer. It should tell your customers about relevant happenings and upcoming new events. Construct them in a way that is quick to read and have all your contact information designed into their newsletter. If they have signed up for the service, most times they will be looking forward to a once a month posting. However, do not make yourself a pest. Do not over populate the email list with daily communications. That is why you use a Blog.

Newsletter notes:
- Always copy and post to your blog.
    o Always create content that is applicable to the reader.
    o Always create content for media outlet publishing differently.
- Creating "quote-able" content that can be published straight into their published local, regional or national compositions.

There is a horde of websites where you can go to publish your own press releases on the internet. Of course, if you can not write

well, then you should not publish. Once on the 'Net, it will follow your career forever.

Hints for press release sites:
- Use that site to release your information. Give it a few days and then Google it for results.
- Use the site that performs best for you.
- Use Alexa.com to show you the rankings of each post.
- *You will find out more information on how to use this service when you go to their website.*

Look at your friends, similar restaurant sites, foodie website and local city-based websites and link to their page. Then back-link to any and all relevant media outlet websites. Back links are all important in the way Google ranks you in their search scoring. The more other people trust the content you

PROVIDE AND DECIDE TO LINK TO YOU, THE MORE SEARCH ENGINES WILL FIND YOU AND BOOST YOUR SITE HIGHER IN PAGE RANKING VISIBILITY.

INDEX:

INDEX:

A

A day in a Life of a South Florida chef 86
Allen Susser 5, 94
Andrea Curto-Randazzo 5, 104
Artist will be Artist 32
Art and Science 25
Augmented Reality 130
Author, Linda Gassenheimer 110
Awestruct Sense, an 79

B

Back to the Future 33
Boundaries and Molds 82
Building a Vibe 42

C

Caribbean 90
Caribbean, Conception 91
Caribbean, Finesse 91
Caribbean, production 92
Chef, Alpha Contemporaries, 90
Chef, Allen Susser 5, 94
Chef, Alice Weingarten 112
Chef Artists 32
Chef Chris Norton 108
Chef Cindy Hutson. 3, 98
Chef Dedication 5
Chef Dewey LaSasso 5, 100
Chef Doug Rodriguez 5
Chef Jan Jorgenson 5, 101
Chef, Mark Millitello 5
Chef Michael Bloise 105
Chef Norman Van Aken 5, 96
Chef Robbin Haas 5
Chefs and Foodies 86
Chefs Andrea and Frank Randazzo 104
Chefs, that have Crafted a Cuisine 89
Chefs, the Thrid Generation 103
Clear and distinct voice 30
Color and light 49
Concerning your Voice 56
Connecting with People 60
Cookery, Formation 18
Cookery, Molds 73
Cookery Processes 28
Cookery Heritages 54
Mastering the Materials 37
Cooking 112
Cooking, Repetition 43
Coupling Flavors 59
Crafted, Cuisine how to 32
Crafted a Cuisine, who has 89
Creativity and Common Sense 81
Cuisine Heritages 49
Culinary Aesthetics 76
Culinary Collections, your recipes 61
Culinary Conception, Alpha's 90
Culinary Future, your 96
Culinary Ideals 28
Culinary Passions 62
Cultivating Ideas 40

D

Day in a life of a South Florida Chef 86
Dedication Page 4-5
Delicious, What if it was easy? 52
Design, weakended 46

Destiny of Ingredients 24
Differences are distinct 38

E

Explaining things 30

F

Facebook 129
Fairchild Gardens 11
Feedly, Google 130
Finesse, Aplha's 78
Flavor Balencing, like deserves like 68
Flavors, brazen bites 70
Flavors 64
Flavor Coupling 65
Flavor, loaned 69
Flavors, real delicious 63
Flavors, simplicity 64
Flavors symmetry 66
Florida, culinary dreamland 10
Florida Fish 11

Florida Foods 12
Food is Art 26
Food, Soul of Food 48
FourSquare 129

G

Google 130

H

How our Cuisine was Crafted 18
How things happen 26

I

Ideas, cultivation 40
Ideas and Ideals 42
Ideas and Ideals, exchanging 45
Ideas, sustenance 36
Ideals, yours 28
Ingredients, natural combinations 66
Ingredients, communion of 74
Internet, who uses 122
Introduction 7

K

Keyword, everything 117
Keyword Loading 117
Knowledge, sharing yours 56

J

Joy of Simplicity 48

L

Like Deserves Like 61
Linda Gassenheimer, author 110
Listen to Inner Self 54
Lite and shade, use of 50
Loaned Flavors 62
Lose the Boundaries 72

M

Mango Events 11
Mango Tasting 12
Mastering the materials 39
Miami 3
Modifying your Ideals 47
Molds, and boundaries 82
Moment please 28

N

New American Riviera 8
New Synthesis, tastes 69
New Times 3
New World Cuisine, NWC cookery 27, 82
Newsletter 133
No-Brainers 81
Nouveau Generation 93

O

Ode to South Florida 20
Organize it 47

P

Pioneering Synthesis 77
Press Release 30, 133

Q

Q.R. Code Usage 126

R

Real-time Media 130
Recipe reation 9
Rules of Old 84

S

Scene as the Vibe 43
Sharing Love of Flavors 57
Simplicity, joy of 48
Simplicity, in the intricate 72
Smart Phone, Apps 125
    Uses 104, 126
Soul of Food 53
Social Media 115
Social Media, Deadly Sins of 123
Social Media, do do these 124
Social Media, Keys 121
Social Media and the Internet 102

Social Media, Keywording 98
Social Media to a Rich Life 121
Social Media, SEO 120
Social Media, Tips on 117
South Florida chef, day in the Life of 86
South Florida, Ode to 20
South Florida twist 10
Sustenance to Ideas 36
Sweetness vs. Subtlety 71
Symmetry of Flavors 66

T

Talent Traits 43
Taste Variance 11
Texture, defiing the dish 49
The Vibe 39
Third Generation Chef 87
Traditions of Cooking 44
Tryst, element of 83

U

Understanding a Chef 33
Understanding Foods 24

V

Value, Garnishing Complexity 75
Vibe, building 42
Vibe, scene as the 43
Voice of a Chef 56
Voice, clear and distinct 30
Voice, concerning Yours 59

W

Weather effects Cooking 37
Win-Win 119
Writing Press Releases 29

Y

Your ,Voice 31
Your, Culinary Collection 55
Your, Culinary Future 115
Your Voice, Your Ideals 51

Remember Chef Michael Bennett's other two book:
"In the Land of Misfits, Pirates and Cooks"
and
"Underneath a Cloudless Sky"

DIRECT WEBLINK TO PURCHASE
MICHAEL'S FIRST BOOK

DIRECT WEBLINK TO PURCHASE
MICHAEL'S SECOND BOOK

Notes:

www.ingramcontent.com/pod-product-compliance
Lightning Source LLC
Chambersburg PA
CBHW061442040426
42450CB00007B/1175